Issues And Your Tissues!

Valerie Miller

References:
Merriam Webster's Collegiate Thesaurus
Copyright ©1988

Microsoft Word, Thesaurus Copyright © 2002
Microsoft Encarta College Dictionary © 2001

Bible References:
All scriptures quotations are referring to the King James
version of the Bible unless otherwise mentioned.

King James Study Bible, Thomas Nelson Inc.
Copyright ©1988

Amplified Bible, Zondervan Copyright ©1987

Women's Devotional Bible 2
New International Version Zondervan Copyright ©1995

*Cover art use with permission from Lulu Self
Publishing, (www.lulu.com)*

Printed In The USA

Dedication

I give all the glory and honor to my Lord, and Savior Jesus Christ. He is the head and deliverer of my life!

To: my lovely daughters Tamaya, Symantha, son William, and to Wadine my mom.

Finally, to all those in bondage, hurting impending freedom this is your season. Be free from your issues now in Jesus name! God Bless You!

Yours in Christ,

Evangelist Valerie Miller

Table Of Contents

Prophesy 5/08/03

I am your healer and your deliverer. In these last days I am going to use you as a channel as well as an instrument to minister to hurting souls. So why are you still sitting back? Write and finish the book, for my people are being destroyed for lack of knowledge.

"Jeremiah 30:2 Thus says the Lord the God of Israel. Write all the words that I have spoken in a Book." (amp)

Revelation 1:11 Saying, I am Alpha and Omega, the first and the last: and, What thou seest, write in a book……. KJV

I Obeyed God!

A Prayer To Prepare!

Father, in the name of Jesus; forgive me for all of my sins as well as short comings. Let me be used for your glory and not for the enemy's device. Let me be a part of your plan and not of a hindrance! Almighty God let me be a blessing in your kingdom and not a curse or a reason for others to pray or stay away. God show me your way and let me not be in the way. Display your Glory and not my pride! Lord let me be a part of your solution and not the problem. Lord make me your instrument and not a distraction. Let me be teachable, reachable, and not skeptical. Lord, be my shield of defense against the adversary his weapons and plans! Don't allow me to be ignorant concerning his devices. Let my eye be single to allow my whole body to be filled with your glorious light of deliverance in Jesus name! Amen!

Introduction

The last 9 years were some difficult years, filled with attacks from the enemy, simply because of this book. **Satan did not want me to write it and neither did I!**

Yet, in order to discuss this needed controversial subject "demon Issues" this would mean exposing some of the skeletons of my past." I just did not want to risk being labeled.

The scripture implying that every knee shall bow and tongue confess that Jesus is Lord seemed appropriate here. Either I bow voluntarily or receive a little help from the Lord. **I got help!**

Saved as well as churched for over 25 years; and at least 12 or more of those years kept in various bondages. Oh yes we shouted practically every service, as well as metaphorically speaking did cart wheels, kicks and tumbles.

Sunday-Sunday my soul was blessed, refreshed but, not secure in deliverance. Meditating on the words, maybe this time I'll be free, but mostly just teased with a spoonful of hope.

To continue, besides from having a big sign on the doorway I observed that most of the ministries I attended then really didn't believe in deliverance. They embraced the doctrinal belief that if you were saved it was <u>impossible</u> for you to have demons.

Because of this, whenever the need to be delivered was mentioned the minister routinely rehearsed the sinner's prayer with me.

Hello, wasn't anybody listening? Wasn't asking to get saved again; didn't have a salvation problem but a bondage problem!

Spending everything I had, including prayer time, efforts, lastly money with expectation. Identifying with the woman with the issue of blood, I had issues and couldn't

9

figure out how to get rid of them, until God showed me how!

To continue, God recently allows me to get set up on my caseworker job to come off of it. Then He mandates me to write this book with no funds or help from anybody but <u>Himself</u>. This seemed totally, unfair. "Doesn't anybody care and, haven't I been through enough!"

Then thinking things over, all the drama, the pain and issues, it was never about me. It was all for His glory so that multitudes would be empowered to be free!

Understand this when the devil had me bound he came to me with everything thought of and he was very raw. Neither did he give a hill of beans about me (nor you the reader). His plans were to kill my credibility as well as bury my influence in this earth. Well God had a better plan for my life and I am forever free!

This is not an ordinary book written just to increase ones head knowledge of deliverance. Neither is it to hear just another inspiring testimony. It is birthed from my own pain and filled with love, as well as unfolded Biblical truths. Designed for extraordinary people, people who are hurting, people who are going through, and want to be free!

My prayer is that the masses out there will open their hearts to receive and be filled with this Rhema Word of God.

MY STORY
AND
DELIVERANCE !

"45 I will walk at liberty: for I seek thy precepts, 46 I will speak of thy testimonies also before kings, and will not be ashamed."

Psalm 119:45-46 KJV

Chapter 1

My Story And Deliverance!

My calling into the deliverance ministry was involuntarily. The Lord, He drafted me. The kicking, protesting *"why me"* could not deter the process. Neither could it excuse any insubordinate behavior. Especially, when He has been too good!

Through the Holy Ghost boot camp, figuratively speaking together with years of rigorous training, these were the workbenches of this present deliverance ministry.

As A soldier in his infantry, Captain Jesus demanded obedience as well as absolute surrender!

Following years of deliverance and brokenness, He

got it. The best thank you Jesus, yes lord, one can give is a life style of obedience. *This book is my yes Lord in action!*

Twenty-five years ago, Jesus became my Savior and during the process my Lord. A gentle soul injured, sexually abused. To continue a second-generational single parent more-over welfare recipient *existing* from government checks. Verbal, as well as physical abuse appeared to be the patterns of my baby daddy selections. The weak choices of men in relationships contributed to my poverty and a single parent household. Yet, it was better to be poor and single than dead.

For years victimized by witchcraft placed on me, and hindered by generational curses. Many years were wasted.

To go on episodes of torments, monstrous images, curses, blasphemes, within my mind resulted in many distressed days, and sleepless nights. The reality of embracing peace seemed subsequently unfeasible then. Often feeling isolated because there was no one to connect to or relate with that understood my dilemma and torments.

Attending school or work was virtually impossible then. Simple tasks such as housecleaning, or even reading a book were troublesome because of the difficulty to focus on the task at hand.

Life then was unbearable because the enemy of my soul was in pursuit to destroy my mind by giving me *his nervous, breakdown!*

Experiencing constant distress and torment of the mind, it became so overwhelming. At times I often begged the Almighty God crying out "Lord make it stop"! Please Lord make it stop"! Hell's imps were living in my body, while tormenting my mind!

Do you know what a blessing it is to have a right mind?

Relatives would come around, offer support, take the children out, to give breaks from time to time out of pity. Pity and monetary gifts could not confer peace of mind. Deliverance was of the essence. My Savior granted me that.

"I'd rather have Jesus than silver and gold". ***Glory Hallelujah! Peace of mind, what's more contentment of heart, is more valuable than anything this world could offer. In my heart, there is a gratefulness resonating, pondering the words. *"Thank you!"*

Deliverance

Being drafted into Gods army presented much opposition. Deliverance required patience and persistence. There was no giving up. Survival depended upon my steadfastness. Throwing the towel in would have resulted in Satan's victory (being committed somewhere). That was not God's will at all.

Rising up early in the morning was a crucial time of combat. For 3 to 5 hours at a time I would lay prostrate on my bedroom floor. To go on, I would recite the Word of God loudly, to override all of the madness in my head.

This was my daily routine, forcefully aiming blows into the enemy's camp in pursuit of my *breakthrough!* Constantly focusing on the Cross of Calvary (hallelujah) yes, the memory of the thorns placed on the Savior's crown, was for *my* peace. Daily communion was often taken as a reminder.

These are some of the scriptures that I confessed:

Isaiah 53:3-5 KJV
3 He is despised and rejected of men; a man of sorrows, and acquainted with grief: and we hid as it were our faces from him; he was despised, and we esteemed him not. 4 Surely he hath borne our griefs, and carried our sorrows: yet we did esteem him stricken, smitten of God, and afflicted. 5 But he was wounded for our transgressions he was bruised for our iniquities: the chastisement of my peace was upon him: and with his stripes we are healed.

Isaiah 26:3 KJV
3 Thou wilt keep him in perfect peace, whose mind is stayed

on thee: because he trusted thee,

Philippians 4:7 KJV
7 And the peace of God which passeth all understanding shall keep your hearts and minds through Christ Jesus.

Mark 11:22-24 KJV
22 And Jesus answering saith unto them, have faith in God. 23 That whosever shall say unto this mountain, Be thou removed, and be Thou cast into the sea: and shall not doubt in his heart, but shall believe that those things which he saith shall come to pass; he shall whatsoever he saith. 24 Therefore I say unto you, What things soever ye desire, when ye pray, believe that ye receive them, and ye shall have them.

The war continued, at night the enemy repetitively made attempts to suffocate me with his demons while I slept. Oftentimes waking up screaming the name of Jesus, these episodes eventually ceased.

The first year or two going to church was most exasperating. Repeatedly, the demons would act up, throw me about during service. To go on, they would have me roll on the floor; push me up against the wall. The saints would plead the blood of Jesus (This would calm the demons but they were still there hiding).

The Lord had mercy on me by allowing me to read faith books by Kenneth E. Hagin Senior. Faith books gave me empowerment to fight. (Thank God for the Late great Kenneth E. Hagin Sr.).

Determined to receive deliverance, testimony service furnished an opportunity to boldly confess God's Word in public. Church folks found it amusing hearing me say, "I thank the Lord for a sound mind"! That was not what they were seeing. Didn't much care what they thought; because God's Words says to call those things that be not as though they already were, Amen! According to my faith so be it! According to my faith it is so now!

You know what's really amazing; saints will believe God for a house a car, the dog, or perhaps a cold to be healed. When it comes to God healing the mind there is a stigma attached to the idea, and lack of faith to believe.

It's like committing the unpardonable sin or having spiritual leprosy. Is there anything too hard for God? *Absolutely not!*

Genuinely convinced of Gods love; absolutely persuaded that, the Devil was the real crazed one. A notice was served to him; it's breaking out time for Valerie Miller. This prison sentence is now over! You will not hold me any more because Jesus paid my bill in full!

A Hostage

Believing enough was placed on my plate, here comes more. When the children were very young, we lived in the Bushwick section of Brooklyn NY.

One morning while doing the breakfast dishes my mother and baby's daddy came over to bring a few dollars, (separately because my mom hated him). Just when she was preparing to leave, mom looked through the peephole assuming she heard sounds outside.

She cracked open the door because the peephole was a bit scratchy. Behind the door was a masked, armed man.

He thrust himself in and yelled "don't nobody move or the children will be killed!" He proceeded by placing his gun to my baby daddy's head; forcing him to tie us up to face 7 hours of terror!

He attempted to violate me, and if I didn't cooperate he threatened to kill me. Not having this rape stuff again. I figured that death couldn't be any worse than my miserable past. I retaliated against his behavior and "In the name of Jesus" is what I said to him!

Astonished, he replied. "What did you say"? Repeating again, "I said In the name of Jesus"! He got up fixed his clothes and as he proceeded to walk away "God loves you" is what I told him. He said, "I know, that's why I am leaving you the h*** alone!"

Unsettled by everything taking place, it was simply too much. Let me die Lord, was my suggestion, (but He would not let me die).

Through all of this he encouraged, and calmed my spirit, reassuring me that everything would be fine. His promise was that one day I will preach His Gospel.

Finally, not knowing who called, the police arrived instantly after the ordeal. It seemed ironic because during that time I didn't have a telephone (simply couldn't afford one).

All the credit goes to God who brought me out over twenty four years ago. Later graduating from college, and was ordained into the ministry. "How about that one *Devil*"? Through all the trials, God has given me much revelation, alongside a mandate to teach, and preach the Gospel. This is my season to do damage to Satan's kingdom; empowering others about deliverance.

Chapter 2

"What Are Issues?"

I mentioned to one of my acquaintances 9 years ago about how I was going to write a book on issues. With sarcasm they remarked "if you got the issues then I got the tissues"!

You got issues is presented as a catchy modern cliché we use on our lovers, family members, enemies or anyone that we do not understand. On the other hand, what about ourselves and what in the world are issues?

According to Microsoft Encarta Dictionary/as well as the Bible, issues has several major meanings.

- **To originate or emergence from,**

For example: Water flows or emerges,

Ezekiel 47:8 KJV
Then said he unto me, These waters issue out toward the east country, and go down into the desert, and go into the sea: which being brought forth into the sea, the waters shall be healed.

- **Offspring, progeny, children, (a baby) a seed**

Isaiah 22:24 KJV
And they shall hang upon him all the glory of his father's house, the offspring and the issue…

Matthew 22:23-25 KJV
23 The same day came to him the Sadducees, which say that there is no resurrection, and asked him, 24 Saying Master, Moses said, If a man die, having no children, his brother shall marry his wife, and raise up seed unto his brother 25 Now there were with us seven brethren: and the first, when he had married a wife, deceased, and having no issue, left his wife unto his brother.

- **Discharge** (fluid from a wound like pus or blood from the body)

A woman during the time of her menstrual cycle was considered unclean because of her issue of blood.

Leviticus 15:19 KJV
And if a woman have an issue, and her issue in her flesh be blood, she shall be put apart seven days: and whosever toucheth her shall be unclean until the even.

Matthew 9:20 KJV
And, behold, a woman which was diseased with an issue of blood twelve years, came behind him, and she touched the hem of his garment:
The book of Leviticus refers to issues as discharges, communicable, and sexually transmitted diseases.

Leviticus 15:2 KJV
Speak unto the children of Israel, and say unto them, When any man hath a running issue out of his flesh, because of the <u>issue</u> he is unclean.

- A Source of flow (Good /or Evil)

Good

God's word tells us that we have to: Keep thy heart with all diligence for out of it are the issues of life. Proverbs 4:23

/or Evil

The Lord began to pour into me revelation about unclean spirits or demonic issues. ***We will discuss more about these issues throughout the book!***

Demons or devils are unholy spirit issues, ungodly seeds; disembodied spirits. They flow through the Dry Places (Matthew 12:43) to get to living bodies, humans/or animals.

Generally, they are incapable to be seen with the naked eye for they are spiritually discerned. For those that are able to discern spiritually, some may appear as a hazy film or fog, diverse in many shapes, figures and sizes.

Although impossible to be seen with the naked eye, many do sense or feel their aura of evil in the atmosphere. Satan has deceived many to believe that what they are feeling is a natural occurrence. In reality, it is a supernatural occurrence.

Through this deception, he uses demon issues to spiritually impregnate mankind to conceive lust and sin.

James 1:15 KJV
Then when lust hath conceived, it bringeth forth sin: and sin, when it is finished, brings forth death.

Are you aware that certain moods, illnesses and personalities can be transferred spiritually?

Have you ever spoken on the telephone and your

head, throat or entire sinus area felt congested. To go on all of a sudden you felt a heaviness or even felt dizzy, or maybe your head began to hurt.

Have you ever listened to a music CD and all of a sudden, you got the love Jones, or even felt depressed? These moods or feelings have happened to many as result of demon issues.

They flow through the airway and transfer via music-telecommunication-man-man-woman or animal.

Modern technology has been one of the factors that contribute to much of this demonic activity released into the atmosphere. Satan the prince of the power of the airway has but a short time on earth. Motivated by his hatred he is using everything he can to contaminate his enemy (mankind).

Revelation 12:12 KJV:
12 Therefore rejoice ye heavens, and ye
that dwell in them. Woe to the inhabiters of the earth and of the sea! For the devil is come down unto you, having great wrath, because he knoweth that he hath but a short time.

The purpose of this book is not to frighten men/or women or make one a fanatic but to enlighten them. Demonic activity is not a myth that one reads about in a story or science fiction book.

Neither is it entertainment that is displayed on TV through cartoons or movies. It is a reality that should not be further *ignored!* Many skip over this area for faith or prosperity messages. To be delivered body, mind, soul, and spirit is the definition of what it means to experience *true prosperity!* 3John 2

Chapter 3

Who Can Have Demons?
(Or Issues)

T his chapter is designed to burst religious, self-righteous bubbles. The devil has lied to the body of Christ. A person _can_ be a Christian or non Christian, and have unclean spirits!

Just look at the news; deacons of churches going on killing sprees, ministers molesting children.

You hear first ladies murdering their husbands, saints loosing their minds and being committed into mental institutions. Saved husbands beating their wives Monday-Saturday and then preach on Sunday. Fornication, homosexuality as well as all types of lasciviousness is running ramped.

Furthermore saved woman are having abortions to go on, saved men and women masturbating. Demonic activity is behind the scenes and is primarily responsible for this lawlessness.

The subject about demons in Christians should not be further ignored. Satan is deceiving humans everywhere. ***Wake up Church!***

Look at Judas:
Luke 22:3 KJV

3 Then <u>entered Satan</u> into Judas surnamed Iscariot, being of the number of twelve. And he went his way, and communed with the chief priests and captains, how he might betray him unto them.

Jesus rebuked the Devil in Peter:
Mark 8:31-33 KJV

31 And he began to teach them, that the
Son of man must suffer many things, and be rejected of the elders, and of the chief priests, and scribes, and be killed, and after three days rise again. 32 And he spake that saying openly. And Peter took him and began to rebuke him. 33 But when he had turned about and looked on his disciples, he rebuked Peter, saying, <u>Get thee behind me</u>, <u>Satan</u>: for thou savourest not the things that be of God, but the things that be of men.

Ananias and Sapphira:
Acts 5:1-3 KJV

1 But a certain man named Ananias, with Sapphira his wife, sold a possession, 2 And kept back part of the price, his wife also being privy to it, and brought a certain part, and laid it at the apostles' feet 3 But Peter said, Ananias <u>why hath Satan filled thine heart</u> to lie to the Holy Ghost, and to keep back part of the price of the land?

The question being asked again, who can have demons? The answer is anyone with a body is a potential target. For Satan, goes about as a roaring lion seeking whom he <u>may</u> devour.

Chapter 4

Holiness And Your Issues!

1 Peter 1:16 KJV
Because it is written, be ye Holy as I am Holy.

T he following is not evidence that one is Holy:
1. Speaking with other tongues.
2. Church membership, attendance and ministry position.
3. Righteous and holy acts.
4. Shouting.
5. Giving up bad habits and sin.

6. The length of ones dress or skirt or the wearing of makeup.
7. How anointed one is.
8. How much money one gives to the church.
9. Not lying, stealing, cursing or swearing.
10. The people one hangs with.
11. With staining from certain meats.
12. Family, and how many years one says they've been saved.

**Religious works and acts will not secure you a place in Heaven you still need to be born again! St John 3:3

- **The definition of holiness is: a state of spiritual soundness and unimpaired virtue**

In other words holiness is the absence of demonic issues, contamination, influence and impurities in ones temple. Not an effort by men but a process being brought forth by the Holy Ghost in men. This is done to make one pure or clean even as God is *pure* and without issues. _This process is called purification or sanctification._

Ephesians 1:23 amp
Which is His body, the fullness of Him Who fills all in all [for in that body lives the full measure of Him Who makes everything complete, and Who fills everything everywhere with Himself]

God wants to fill us with himself. Holiness is who he is. He uses our _lifetime_ to bring our body and souls to the level of complete submission as well as unimpaired holiness to be (issue free). Until this process is completed, we have Gods grace in the areas of weakness.

Ephesians 2:8 KJV
For by grace we are ye saved through

faith, and not of yourselves: it is the gift of God not of works lest any man should boast.

Holiness is the absence of sin, and God alone has the power to make one Holy! It is achieved only by the Holy Ghost not self righteous works!

Zechariah 4:6 KJV
6 Then he answered and spake unto me saying, This is the word of the Lord unto Zerubbabel, Not by might, nor by power, but by my spirit saith the Lord of host.

The Holy Ghost
You don't catch the Holy Ghost as if you do a cold. You do not get the Holy Ghost because you are clean or good. He is received by faith (because good people can have demon issues and struggles).

I was taught that if you are in living in sin you are playing church if you shout during service. *That's a lie especially if the anointing is present. The anointing is for your struggles. You can not do it alone; you do need God as your helper.*

Hebrew 13:6,
6 So that you we may boldly say, The Lord is my helper, and I will not fear what man shall do unto me.

The more you get dive into the anointing and apply it while it is flowing, the more shackles and yokes to be removed and destroyed. If you are loosened than you can walk out of captivity more *easily.* Isaiah 61:1

The Holy Ghost is also present to fill you, to assist you, to teach, cleanse, purge, and help you kick demons (squatters) out of your temple. To make you more like God. He also comforts you because sanctification can be a little unpleasant.

John 14:26 KJV
26 But the Comforter, which is the Holy Ghost, whom the Father will send in my name, he shall teach you all things, and bring all things to your remembrance, whatsoever I have said unto you.

Legal Rights Of Possession!

Transference (Issues)

Chapter 5

Legal Rights Of Possession!
(Transference Issues)

S atan is an imitator in addition to being the Father of all liars. He assigns his workers to spiritually impregnate humans with issues through *ignorance* as well as willful acts of sin.

John 10:10 KJV
The thief cometh not but for to steal, and to kill and to destroy...

Not caring who you are, a mother, a father, a child, rich or poor, he just wants a body legally/or illegally. Empathizing on *illegal* because he is a thief, and he does not care much about laws. Regardless to say criminals, even Satan and his imps have rights and are quite aware of them.

Legal Rights

There are laws governing the kingdom of darkness and light. Just because we don't know them all, Satan is not at all ignorant concerning his rights. For that reason God will not go against his word under any stipulations. God's word is binding and legal. When Adam and Eve sinned in the garden it threw the whole foundation of the Earth out of course according to Ps. 82:5. If God were to lie, it would not only further place the foundations of Heaven and Earth out of course, they would cease to exist!

Great is His faithfulness. Oftentimes Christians are deceived because the enemy has blinded their eyes. (As discussed in a previous chapter) he deceives many to believe that saints cannot have evil spirits.

While it is illegal for them to be in a believer's body, many do struggle with unclean spirits because of *ignorance* and *sin*. Many are also ignorant of Laws of transference.

For this cause I am privileged to share what was revealed to me many years ago.

Leviticus 11:1-8 KJV
1 And the Lord spake unto Moses and Aaron, saying unto them, 2 speak unto the children of Israel saying, These are the beasts which ye shall eat among all the beast that are on the earth. 3 Whatsoever parteth the hoof, and is cloven footed, and cheweth the cud among the beast, that shall ye eat. 4 Nevertheless these shall ye not eat of them that chew the cud, or of them that divideth not the hoof he is unclean unto you. 5 And the coney, because he cheweth the cud, but divideth not the hoof; he is unclean you. 6 And the hare, because he cheweth the cud but divideth not the hoof he is unclean unto you. 7 And the swine, though he divideth the

hoof, and be cloven footed, yet he divideth cheweth not the cud he is unclean to you. 8 Of their flesh shall ye not eat, and their carcass shall ye not touch they are unclean to you.

The writer Moses gives details about the Levitical laws that were assigned by God concerning diet for the people of God under the old covenant.

According to verse three they were forbidden to eat animals that did not have clothen feet, split hoofs, and chew the cud.

The animals had to do all or they were forbidden to eat or even touch. Unlawful animals were also called unclean, or common. Even their deceased bodies were an abomination to God.

Leviticus 11:43-47 KJV

43 Ye shall not make yourselves abominable with any creeping thing that creepeth, neither shall ye make yourselves unclean with them, that ye shall be defiled thereby. 44 For I am the Lord your God: ye shall therefore sanctify yourselves, and ye shall be holy; for I am holy: neither shall ye defile yourselves with any manner of creeping thing that creepeth upon the earth. 45 For I am the Lord that bringeth you up out land of Egypt, to be your God: ye shall therefore be holy, for I am holy. 46 This is the law of the beasts and of the fowl, and of every living creature that moveth in the waters, and every creature that creepeth upon the earth 47 To make a difference between the unclean and the clean, and the beast that may be eaten and the beast that may not be eaten.

As mentioned in a previous chapter, Holiness is the absence of sin. It is also purity being free from demon issues, (uncommon or clean). Verse 45 expresses that Holiness is who God is. Furthermore verse 47 informs us that there are animals that were ceremonially clean or unclean.

Revelation

Laws of Holiness were more than just mere dietary laws for health purposes. These laws served as a protection for God's people to keep them free from demonic transference issues.

It was forbidden for Gods people to even touch unclean animals especially their carcasses. For, whenever the demons exited the deceased bodies they sought the nearest victim to *renter* into.

These laws, principles and boundaries in the spirit world, were also set up to make a distinction between what animals demons were permitted to enter into and forbidden. Again verse 47 calls them the unclean and the clean animals.

Satan and his imps knew about the laws of unclean animals in which they had permission to enter. Let me give you an example from the Word of God.

Mark 5:2-13 KJV

2 And when he was come out of the ship, immediately there met him out of the tombs a man with an unclean spirit 3 Who had his dwelling among the tombs; and no man could bind him, no, not with chains: 4 Because that he had been often bound with fetters and chains, and the chains had been plucked asunder by him, and the fetter broken in pieces: neither could any man tame him. 5 And always, night and day, he was in the mountains and in the tombs, crying, and cutting himself with stones. 6 But when he saw Jesus afar he ran and worshiped him. 7 And cried with a loud voice, and said, what have I to do with thee Jesus, thou Son of the most high God? I adjure thee by God that thou torment me not.

The demons recognized Jesus and, became terrified, worried of their doom!

Mark 5:8-10 KJV

8 For he said to him, Come out of the man, thou unclean spirit. 9 And he asked him, What is thy name? And he answered saying, My name is Legion: for we are many.

10 And he besought him much that he would not send him out of the country.

The truth of the matter is, although they confessed to Jesus that their name was *Legion* but one of their other names was *Region*. Fearful that Satan their master would punish them by making a spectacle out them for incompletion of their territorial regional assignment. They asked Jesus to let them stay.

Mark 5:11-13 KJV
11 Now there was there nigh unto the mountains a great herd of swine feeding. 12 And all the devils besought him saying, Send us into the swine, that we may enter into them, 13 And forthwith Jesus gave them leave. And the unclean spirits went out and entered into the swine.

Guess what the Savior had to honor their request because this was (The Law of the Beast and the Fowl.... **Lev 11:46**) Or Possession, and Transference concerning animals that demons legally could enter into.

Because swine were unclean *then,* they had a right to enter!

Other unclean animals
All animals that do not have split, hooves and chew the cud. Animals like rodents, animals with paws such as, cats, dogs, Lions, tigers and bears.

Frogs were unclean, Revelation 16:13 KJV
13 And I saw three unclean spirits like frogs come out of the mouth of the dragon, and out of the mouth of the beast, and out of the mouth of the false prophet. For they are the spirits of devils, working miracles, which go forth unto the kings of the earth and of the whole world, to gather them to the battle of that great day of God Almighty.

Some examples of more unclean and clean animals

Unclean animals
Every animal that does not have split hooves and does not chew the cud,
The camel
The coney
The swine
The hare

Clean animals
Every animal that has split hooves and chews the cud
The deer
The cow
The giraffe
The goat
The lamb
The sheep

Some examples of unclean and clean birds

Unclean birds	Clean birds
These are detestable:	The chicken
The eagle	The dove
The suffrage	The turkey
The ospray	
The kite	
The falcon	
The raven	
The ostrich	
The nighthawk	
The sea gull	
The owl	
The ibis	
The vulture	
The swan	
The pelican	
The stork	
The bat	

Some samples of unclean and clean insects

Unclean insects	Clean insects
All winged insects,	Some beetles
that have four feet	Grasshoppers
	The cricket
	The Locust

*See Leviticus 11:1-31 for the complete list including fish.

**Take note
This list of animals, insects, fish and fowl is only to show a spiritual distinction of the Levitical laws. It's not saying to the Christian or unbeliever not to eat them. I am not teaching any doctrine but spiritual principles, as well as laws.

1 Tim 4:4-5 amp
4 For every creature of God is good and nothing is to be thrown away or refused if it is received with thanksgiving.
5 For it is hallowed and consecrated by the Word of God and by prayer.

Verse 5 For it is made hallow or holy by the Word of God, what Word of God was Timothy referring to?

Acts: 10:11-15 amp
11 And he saw the sky opened and something like a great sheet lowered by the four corners, descending to the earth. 12 It contained all kinds of quadrupeds and wild beast and creeping things of the earth and birds of the air. 13 And there came a voice to him, saying, Rise up Peter, kill and eat. 14 But Peter said, No by no means, Lord: for I have never eaten anything that is common and unhallowed or [ceremonially] unclean.

Verse 15 is the Word of God that Timothy was referring to.

> ➢ 15 And the voice came to him again a second time, <u>What God has cleansed and pronounced clean, do not you defile and profane by regarding and calling common and unhallowed or un-clean.</u>

The Lord Jesus Christ fulfilled these laws through his death, burial, and resurrection. The lawless one, the one who works iniquity on this earth continues to violate these laws John 10:10! As long you pray and offer thanksgiving, you are free from defilement and issues during mealtime.

Transference in Christians:

As mentioned before demons do not have legal rights to enter in Christians unless they give them that right through sin or ignorance. 2 Cor. 2:11.

Many individuals entertain spirits because they just do not know any better. Oftentimes they do not know how to get rid of them.

Demons knew that it was illegal to enter into Jesus. He was the perfect lamb sacrifice with no guile or lies found in his mouth. Never did he give place to the Devil. (We don't have to either). Satan has nothing in Him that he wants. His holy, issue free blood paid for our redemption as well as liberty in full! We are kept complete in Christ.

St John 14:30 amp

30 I will not talk with you much more, for the prince (evil genius, ruler) of the world is coming. And he has no claim on Me. [He has nothing in common with Me; there is nothing in Me that belongs to him, and he has no power over Me].

Guess what we have the same right to be free from issues, of torment, sickness, lust etc!

1 John 4:17 KJV
Herein is our love made perfect, that we may have boldness in the day of judgment: because as he is, so are we in this world.

Confession

Lord, I repent of my ignorance and of all my sins. Jesus come into my life and be my Savior and lord. I thank you for saving me. I declare according to Matthew 18:18 it to be unlawful, illegal, and improper for demons or devils to transfer into me or any one of my family members in the name of Jesus. I have the right to be free and protected against all transference spirits. Even as Jesus was in this earth, free from oppression, depression, rejection, and possession and every other foul spirit. Because of the blood of Jesus and the cross of Calvary I am now free. I know the word Satan and the Son of God have truly made me free indeed. Amen!

Matthew 12:43 amp
43 But when the unclean spirit has gone out of a man, it roams through dry [arid places] in search of rest, but it does not find any.

Luke 11:24 amp
24 When the unclean spirit has gone out of a person it roams through, waterless places in search of rest (release, refreshment, ease) and finds none it says, I will go back to my house from which I came.

Chapter 6

Demon Issues
(Dry Places)

T his chapter will discuss demon issues in Dry Places. The writer Matthew expresses how unclean spirits leave out of a man. He doesn't mention whether they were cast out or just left on their own for transference purposes. When they left they roamed around awhile. Where did they roam? Dry, arid, waterless or (lifeless) places, that's where.

What are Dry Places?

The Dictionary/Thesaurus defines dry as waterless, devoid, deficient in moisture, arid, barren, and UN garnished.

Because these two verses and reference definitions were unclear to me, I asked the Lord to give me understanding. Often hearing other believers binding, casting out demons and sending them to the Dry Places I wondered, "What are these places"? He began teaching me that Dry Places are temporally dwelling places for demon spirits. A Dry Place is any molecular, lifeless (non-breathing) non-living, temporary instrument, object, substance that demons can travel through to get to a permanent host body. A Solid, liquid or gas can be a Dry Place. Water is wet in the natural sense but a Dry Place in the spiritual sense because it falls under the above description. See Leviticus 11:36, 38 about water becoming unclean.

They are also paper, fabric, wood, metal, cement, plastic, food, and more.

Leviticus 11:31-32 amp
31 These are unclean to you among all that creep; whoever touches them when they are dead shall be unclean until evening. 32 An whatever they may fall when they are dead, whether it is an article of wood or clothing or skin (bottle) or sack,

These are vehicles that Satan and his imps use to get to a host body, human/ or animal. It doesn't matter whether it is a religious item with markings or symbols. Neither if it's a pair of white or blue socks thrown in the bottom of the closet. The enemy doesn't care he just needs a vehicle to get to a body!

Let's discuss some of these Dry Places.

Paper, books, money

People handle money including people that are contaminated with spirit issues. Through these items, spirits are circulated around the world.

Old used fabrics, sheets, blankets curtains, shoes, and clothing **See Leviticus 15 verses 5-8.

Of my early years being a Christian, the Lord dealt with me about taking clothing from different people. Being a victim of poverty we were very limited with funds to buy new clothes. Family, friends and, church members donated much of what was owned. The old apartment was constantly flooded with bags of used clothing and shoes. Not to seem ungrateful, some of these items were like new, beside from being very nice. In addition to the clothing and the clutter along came the spirits the former owners were struggling with. God told me to "throw them out"!

Why? Spiritual depression had entered into my home through the clothing along with suicide, poverty, fear confusion etc. Satan for many years had used this as a channel to contaminate my home.

Spirits love to attach to clutter especially clothing because of the ability to hide there. Take note washing the clothing will not alone remove spirits they must be blessed and prayed over.

(A positive point)

God's Spirit or anointing can permeate and bless cloths, aprons, handkerchiefs, oil to heal as well as cast out demons.

Acts 19:11-12 KJV

And God wrought special miracles by the hand of Paul: 12 So that from his body were brought unto the sick handkerchiefs or aprons, and diseases departed from them, and the evil spirits went out of them.

Wood, plaster, cement, furniture

Spirits issue through furniture, sofas, tables, chairs, desks.

Mattresses **See Leviticus 15 verses 5-8

Envision an old used or refurbished mattress brought from a thrift shop. If the original owners suffered for many years with lustful, depression spirits etc. You can just about imagine what the new owners might experience. Let the buy beware!

Staffs, rods and canes
Exodus 7:11-12 KJV

11 Then Pharaoh also called the wise men and the sorcerers: now the magicians of Egypt, they also did in like manner with their enchantments. 12 for they cast down every man his rod and they became serpents: but Aaron's rod swallowed up their rods.

This may seem extreme but it gives a Biblical demonstration of how spirits can transfer into objects.

Buildings and walls

Living in many apartment complexes including the projects has been a job in itself. It seems as if more time was spent on trying to keep the apartment spiritually clean rather than physically clean.

Demons have easy access to travel through walls, floors, and ceilings. At times while in the living room relaxing God enabled me to see a light hazy film or feel a heaviness pervade through the walls. Whatever the neighbors were doing would affect my home if, I did not take authority immediately over the atmosphere.

Upon interviewing friends they had similar

experiences in their apartments.

Elizabeth: was in her kitchen one day; all of a sudden, she felt a strange feeling along with a heaviness come through the walls to her apartment. She looked through the peephole of the door and saw a strange man using drugs in the hallway.

Vicki: lived in her grandmother's house on the third floor. Vicki was a born again believer for three years. One evening while asleep she awoke startled in the middle of the night. She felt the sensation of hands all over her, and it felt as if she was being molested. She attempted to go back to sleep but after the episode but had trouble doing it. Later about five in the morning Vicki heard banging on the wall. It was her drunken neighbor banging on the wall begging to come into her room to have sex with her. Vicki was frightened and refused to open the door. Eventually he stopped. He apologized the next day explaining that he did not know what came over him, and that he was drunk (whatever). To go on yes, evil spirits including lust can transfer through the walls because walls are *Dry Places*!

Dust and dirt

Cleanliness is next to Godliness. Is not just a saying but of a truth. Spirits love to attach to and journey through dust and dirt to settle in individual's homes. When the disciples were not received they were told to shake the dust off their feet. Math 10:14, Luke 10:11, In other words get rid of the spiritual negativity. A foot washing was a courtesy as well as a necessity because during that time there were no trains or buses but dirt roads.

Oftentimes dirt is associated with poverty, crime, underdeveloped countries, crowded cities as well as *depression!*

Housecleaning

Many spiritualists as well as saved folks believe that

they can drive demons out of their homes using candles, incense, smelly oils, bleach or ammonia.

About 4 years ago, I was helping this little church out. A woman named Carmen was a member there (not her real name). She was able to speak in beautiful tongues even knew the word inside out. Carmen invited us to her home so we went my daughter and me. Upon arrival, we observed an altar of candles and incense in the middle of the floor.

Inquiring out of curiosity, "what in the world is it that"? "Why do you need to do this"? "Isn't the Blood of Jesus and His name enough"! She brought up something about the Yoruba religion, expressing that the candles and incense are for housecleaning and removal of unclean spirits. Beside that, she said, "Jesus told her to do it". What Jesus was the real question? All of a sudden, a strange presence filled the room.

Carmen gave me the evil eye, then took this big pan, lit some incense and began shaking it around house. That was my sign to get my happy self out of there. She was a *witch!*

Believers need only to use the blood, the name of Jesus, alongside their God given authority to pray using the anointed Word of God to cleanse, and seal their homes! A life style of holiness together with obedience will also add weight to ones prayer.

Our weapons are not fleshly. Using religious candles, a Spiritualist, witchcraft prayers, incense, cultic masks, statues of Mary and Jesus will only attract unclean spirits.

The book of James says submit yourself therefore to God resist the devil and he will flee from you! (The legal way)

Metal
Utensils, pots, pans, wiring, coins

Leviticus 11:31, 35 amp
31 These are unclean to you among all that creep; whoever touches them when they are dead shall be unclean to the

evening. 35 And everything upon which any part of their carcass falls shall be unclean; whether an <u>oven</u>, or <u>pan</u> with a <u>lid</u> or <u>hearth</u> for <u>pots</u>,

Wiring:

Any cable wiring,

Telecommunication including

The television, telephone, and the computer:

Have you ever viewed a movie or conversed on the telephone and suddenly your head ached or you felt congested in your throat or head area. Maybe all of a sudden you felt dizzy, unfocused, tired or a heaviness on your back and shoulders? Thought it was you huh, but you noticed whenever you called certain individuals, you felt these same symptoms. For years, you believed it was sinus.

These are issues passing through the telecommunication systems by way of (contaminated individuals). Because of modern technology, we are privileged to see and experience from all over the world what was impossible to even imagine 25-50 years ago. Television, computers, VCR'S, CD'S, DVD'S, cable, including satellite, enable us to view just about anything 24/7. Not only do individuals receive the movie, music, or the message, but the actual spirits. No, I am not glorifying the devil but informing the consumers. Be alert the enemy is setting up his kingdom in homes even Christian homes (maybe yours)!

To: all you young or young at heart that love secular hip-hop music. Furthermore heavy metal, rock and roll, music videos, some (Christian music) beware! Much of this music may be reproducing spirits after their own kind lust, fear, hate, as well as murder. The Devil is strategically using electronic devices to set up strongholds in the minds of many.

When strongholds spirits are set up it is difficult to receive the flow of the anointing. The reason is you cannot put new wine in old wine skins that are filthy clogged up or contaminated. A river of Life cannot flow when there is a dam or blockage full of issues.

The Internet

Perverted, as well as pornographic spirits, transfer via the Internet into millions of homes all over the world daily.

Many patrons become addicted to the Internet chat rooms even Instant Messaging using the cell phone picking up spirits in the process.

Food

Haggai 2:12-13(amp)

12 If one carries in the skirt of his garment flesh that is holy [because it has been offered a sacrifice to God] and with his skirt or the flaps of his garment he touches bread, or pottage or wine, or oil, or any kind of food, does what he touches become holy [dedicated to God's service exclusively]? And the priest answered, No Holiness is not infectious.

In other words, Holiness is not something you can catch or be transferred. An anointed cloth or eating anointed food cannot make you fit for heaven. You still need to be Born Again, and during this time when Haggai recorded these verses the whole law had to be observed.

13 Then said Haggai, If one who is [ceremonially] unclean? because he has come in contact with a dead body should touch these articles of food, shall it be [ceremonially) unclean? And the priest answered, It shall be unclean. [Unholiness is infectious.]

In both passages the word *infectious* is a word that also means *transferable* according to the Dictionary/Thesaurus in MS Word. Unholiness or unholy spirits are transferable.

Contaminated individuals preparing meals can ignorantly transfer unclean spirits to the food or drink.

**Take note the longer the individual preparing the food lingers around the food the more probable the items to be contaminated. In New York there are hundreds of bodega corner stores as well as chicken restaurants.

Whenever I would enter a store and just so happened to hear cultic music playing I would leave in the past.
The reason: much of this music is satanically anointed.
When it is released it permeates throughout the store.
Whatever spirits were reproduced through the music like fornication, depression, murder, witchcraft etc it is now in the merchandise or food.

Some Eastern religion restaurants even have altars that include fruit above their counters.

1 Corinthians 8:1(KJV)
Now as touching things offered into idols…

Revelation 2:14(KJV)
14 But I have a few things against thee, because thou hast there them that hold the doctrine of Balaam, who taught Balac to cast a stumblingblock before the children
of Israel, to eat things sacrificed unto idols and to commit fornication.

When in doubt concerning the status of the food you're eating pray! As a matter a fact pray over everything that enters your temple.

1 Timothy 4:4-5 KJV
4 Every creature of God is good, and nothing to be refused, if it be received with thanksgiving: The fifth verse says, for it is sanctified by the word of God and prayer.

The Airway:
Amplifiers, Musical instruments, Wireless devices, Satellite devices

Ephesians 2:2 amp
In which at one time you walked [habitually]. You were following the course and fashion of this world [were under the sway of the tendency of this present age], *following the prince of the air* [You were obedient to and under the control of] the [demon] spirit that still constantly works in the sons of disobedience [the careless, the rebellious, and the unbelieving, who go against the purposes of God].

Satan who is the prince of the power of the airway causes many to become bound through thought and demonic influence. Using ammunitions of strongholds, he infuses the airway with depression, loneliness, fear, worry, oppression and demonic illnesses etc. He is in charge of all the demonic issue energy, the filth that is assigned to hinder the people of God to keep them defeated, spotted and unholy.

Wireless and satellite devices
When signals are picked up the spirit attached may be good or evil. No matter how far away the signal has traveled the spirits attached can be transferred right into ones home.

Chapter 7

Classifications
Of Spirits!

Psalms 8:3-6 KJV
3 When I consider thy heavens, the work of thy fingers, the moon and the stars, which thou hast ordained; 4 what is man that thought art mindful of him? And the son of man, that thou visitest him? 5 For thou hast made him a little lower than the angels, and hast crowned him with glory and honor. 6 Thou madest him to have dominion over the works of thy hands: thou hast put all things under his feet:

There are two major classifications of spirits: *Holy* as well as *Evil!*

Holy spirits

God
Is a Holy Spirit
He is also called The Holy Ghost
The Almighty God, The Word The Almighty Creator, and Ruler of the Universe.
God's angels, sons of God
They are holy spirits, The Heavenly host
Job 2:1
Born Again Christians
They have holy spirits because their spirits are born of God by receiving and accepting Jesus Christ as savior. They are also sons of god. St John 1:12

Evil spirits

Satan
Is an evil spirit, because he is a fallen angel resulting from his lawlessness or (iniquity), an ex son of god. He is the ruler of darkness of this world and age.
The 1/3 Fallen angels
Are evil spirits because they are ruled by Satan, they are ex sons of god. (The believers now have their vacant positions as sons of god) Man benefited because of the fall. These evil spirits principalities powers, spiritual wickedness in high places contribute to, helping reinforce the lawlessness on earth.
Witches and Warlocks
They are also evil spirits because they choose to serve Satan. They have an evil heart. They cast spells that are orchestrated and then accomplished by demons. They also help influence, and enforce lawlessness by doing so.
Demons
They are devils, disembodied evil spirits that are searching for a host body. They are the spirit issues that attack mankind in different ways to fulfill the assignments of Satan. For example: spirits of infirmities, depression, lust, compulsive disorders, and behaviors, confusion, laziness, procrastination etc. Some say they are the fallen angels or the came from pre Adamic period, but all I know is that they are evil!

To appoint unto them that mourn in Zion, to give unto them beauty for ashes, the oil of joy for mourning, the garment of praise for the <u>spirit of heaviness;</u>...........that he might be glorified. **Isaiah 61:3**

Chapter 8

The Spirit Of Heaviness!

R ight here I am going discuss one of the major demon spirits that is affecting mankind, the spirit of heaviness or spiritual depression. This spirit is being released on man more now than ever. Much of this has resulted from witchcraft spells released into the atmosphere. It's in the air and it transfers through the walls, telephone, music, and television. You find it in schools, work places, families, Churches etc.

Having suffered from spiritual depression for many years, in addition to interviewing others equipped me with insight to recognize some signs.

Spiritual depression is a thick heaviness, a dark cloud that positions itself on and in individuals. It becomes a part of their aura bringing the blues, sadness, loneliness, and hopelessness. One may feel tired frequently.

During the years, I saw many individuals so bound up it appeared as if they were in a trance.

There are different levels of spiritual depression. If the person doesn't resist but chooses to entertain it, they will fall deeper and deeper into its clutches. Eventually their strength and will to fight is exhausted. Satan will even make up things or blow up situations in their mind to the extreme that they might say *why bother with life let me die.*

This demon can influence the appetite. The sufferer can either overeat or become anorexic. Everyone anorexic is not trying to lose weight neither is afraid of food.

Individuals under attack by spiritual depression may feel caught off guard. Under a strong delusion or deception they're often persuaded by the enemy's hopeless lies.

My suggestion is to be prepared when he returns by having a plan of action in between attacks. Build a fortress of the Word of God in your heart Psalm 119:11, Psalm 144:2, Col 3:15.

.....*Resist the devil, and he will flee from you.*
James 4:7 KJV

Chapter 9

How Do Spirits Enter?

Turn to Matthew 12:43 amp
When the unclean spirit has gone out of a man, it roams through dry [arid places] in search of rest, but it does not find any.

<u>Now let us examine</u> **Luke 11:24** *in the amplified version:* When the unclean spirit has gone out of a person it roams through, waterless places in search of rest (<u>release, refreshment, ease</u>): and finding none it says, I will go back to my house from which I came.

U nclean spirits (demons) are (disembodied), without a natural body. That is why they seek one for release, expression and personality in the physical. They cannot find it in the air, paper, metal, wood, food, fabric, or any other Dry Place as discussed in an earlier chapter. These are only vehicles to get to a host body, be it human/or animal. Unclean spirits roam through dry, lifeless places because they are not satisfied.

They only get refreshment and satisfaction when they are in a living body. This is where they can contaminate, corrupt, and implant their ungodly issue seeds to fulfill Satan's assignments. They get a kick out of making man/or woman's life a living nightmare. They are not at ease or rest until they obey their master's plan.

During the years the Lord gave me discernment to see spirits and I have discussed this topic with others that have also seen them.

I asked God. "Where do spirits get their current shape"? He revealed "that many came from the last body they entered whether it was an animal or human being or mixture."

Turn to Revelation 16:13-14 amp
13 And I saw three loathsome *spirits* like *frogs,* [leaping] from the mouth of the dragon and from the mouth of the beast and from the mouth of the false prophet. 14 For really they are the spirits of demons that perform signs wonders, miracles). And they go forth to the rulers and leaders all over the world, to gather them together for war the great day of God Almighty.

In this passage the last shape of the host body was that of a frog. In a previous chapter, we discussed the Leviticus laws concerning clean and unclean animals.

If they didn't chew the cub and split the hoof, or list as clean in Lev 11, the animals were unfit for ceremonial use. They were considered unholy. Examples were rats, frogs, snakes, dogs, and swine. Demons had legal permission to enter into these animals. Demons prefer humans because they are the dominant species on earth. Invading host bodies for rest, release of expression, refreshment and ease. They are like fleas that feed off of blood and skin.

Demons roam through Dry Places endlessly. They

often connect with and hide in clothing, metal and all non-living things to get to _you_ a body.

Satan loves trying to imitate Gods creative power. _Remember in Isaiah 14 that he wanted to be like God_. His ultimate goal is to contaminate mankind.

He is doing this by infusing mankind with demons through transference, body to body whether it be human or an animal.

Entrances of the Body

Entering through different channels they mix with saliva, mucus and form a sheave covering. This is done in order that they cover different parts of the body organs and systems. They place blockages in many areas, as well as cloud the vision and focus.

Demons were around way before mankind was created. They were able to study the earth and the anatomy of the various bodies whether human or animal.

**Please take note I am in no wise trying to diagnose any sickness, illness or disease. If you are suffering from or showing signs of a disabling illness seek a medical professional.

Unclean spirits enter through the following channels, to contaminate the body!

The eyes

They enter in and travel to the back of the eye area as a result of the victim being in a contaminated environment.

The nose

They enter through the nasal area as a result of the individual being in a contaminated environment. They cause congestion, as well as blockages. It may interfere with speaking, singing and breathing.

The ears

They also enter into the individual by way of being in a contaminated room or around contaminated persons.

Lust and other spirits can transfer through the telephone. Headphone devices including the telephone operate as a spiritual intravenous needle. They cause demons entering through the wiring (Dry Places) to go directly into the body by way of the ear! Soul ties can be formed by unholy relationships through the telephone. Examples are: Phone sex, (spiritual prostitution, or spiritual whoring).

The throat

They enter through the mouth, through French kissing, oral sex, and eating food or drink that have been contaminated by unclean spirits. They are swallowed and imparted in the stomach and transferred to different parts of the body.

Individuals may experience feelings of hopelessness, depression, lack of concentration or confusion. Sometimes poor choices for friends can make one a sponge for demons.

The sexual organs

They mix with female or male secretions entering, through the mouth, ear, male sex organs, the rectum, and female sex organs. They travel in the body causing impartation around the sexual organs.

We interviewed many women that were going through in their flesh. They would share with me how they sometimes felt something wrapping around their ovaries or fallopian tubes causing pain. These demons cause the individuals to be in total bondage to lustful sexual appetites in addition to all types of lasciviousness including homosexual acts.

Many masturbate have orgies, for release in addition to all other types of promiscuous acts. The only thing that seems to matter is that the flesh be satisfied. Many are raped in the spirit because of ungodly soul ties.

The pores

Unclean spirits fumigate through the pores of the skin and empty into the blood stream and other systems in the body. They are reciprocated through touch, from rubbing too close to people in public places. Examples: trains, buses, or crowded places.

They also hide and transfer through Dry Places like clothing, furniture, money, jewelry, oils. An example: years ago I would buy sterling silver earrings from street vendors. Every time I would wear the jewelry I would feel a heaviness or get a headache. The Lord informed me it was the earrings. This would happen until I either prayed over the earrings or stopped wearing them. The same thing would happen to me with scented oils purchased off the street.

(In reference to the Old Testament) because unclean spirits entered through touch the people of God were forbidden to touch dead bodies. Anything that touched the dead body those items were contaminated and considered unlawful, or unclean!

Haggai 2:13 amp
13 Then said Haggai, If one who is (ceremonially) unclean because he has come in contact with a dead body should touch any of these articles of food, shall it be [ceremonially] unclean? And the priest answered, It shall be unclean. [Unholiness is infectious.]

Leviticus 11:31-32 KJV
31 These are unclean to you among all that creep; whosoever doeth touch them, when they be dead, shall be unclean until the even. 32 And upon whatsoever any of them, when they are dead, doth fall, it shall be unclean; whether it be any vessel of wood, or raiment, or skin, or sack, whatsoever vessel it be, wherein any work is done, it must be put into water and it shall be unclean until the even; so it shall be cleansed.

For God speaks in his word;

2 Corinthians 6:17 KJV
Wherefore come out from among them, and be ye separate, saith the Lord, and touch not the unclean thing; and I will receive you.

Colossians 2:21 KJV
Touch not; Taste not; handle not;

The blood:
The life of every animal and human is in the blood. God was very strict about blood contamination in the Old Testament. Blood is often contaminated through demon issues; inherited curses as well as spirits of infirmities. Leviticus 17:7, 11

Spirits are inherited through the blood and DNA.

Ezekiel 18:2 KJV
What mean ye, that ye use this proverb
concerning the land of Israel saying, The fathers have eaten sour grapes and the children's teeth are set at edge?

St John 9:1-2 KJV
1 And as Jesus passed by, he saw a man which was blind from his birth. 2 And his disciples asked him, saying
Master, who did sin, this man, or his parents, that he was born blind?

Spirits circulate thru the body and flow from organ to organ via the circulatory as well as other systems in the body. They connect to body tissues, like the heart, liver stomach, knees, joints, back, eyes, brain etc. They hide in the bone marrows, joints, as well as connective tissues.

Hebrews 4:12-13 KJV
The word of God is quick and powerful and sharper than any

two edge sword, piercing even to the dividing asunder of soul and spirit and of the <u>joints</u>, and <u>marrow</u> and intents of the heart. Neither is there any creature that is not manifest in his sight.

Let us look at this verse 12 in more detail. The Word of God is quick and powerful and sharper than any two edge sword…, It divides asunder of the marrow, (Bone marrow), (Joints), (connective tissues). Why does the Word do this? Answer, the anointed Word does this do to bring deliverance to the individual. Unclean spirits hide in the bone marrow where red blood cells are stored. They also hide in organs, tissues and joints.

God's anointed Word according to verse 13 it is a light and brings every creature to be manifest in his sight. God wants our body, soul and spirit to be sanctified <u>*wholly*</u>!

Sex And Other Related Issues!

The Lord is thy Keeper…

Psalm 121:5 KJV

Chapter 10

Sex And Other Related Issues!

Fourteen years ago I was bound up in a prison cell of fornication. In the mist of preparing to indulge again, suggesting that my partner to use a condom because getting pregnant was not an option.

God said to me "the man you are getting ready to lay with is not your husband and you are on your way to hell if you don't stop it. In addition to this you should be more afraid of sexually transmitted demons and getting pregnant with them!"

Disobedient as I was during the time I still became intimate with him. That evening I noticed how bloated my stomach had become just as if I was 3 months pregnant. Later vomiting this white foam; my stomach became empty. The lord ministered to me that this was the result of fornicating with this man.

These were his demons that were deposited in you. "I will not allow you to continue in this you will be *holy*"! (I repented)

People that Fornicate or commit Adultery often pick up a false worldly favor called *the spirit of seduction*. If not repented and cast out of the individual; it can be transferred to others including the congregation through ministering!

Abortion, an Option or a Sacrifice?

Many Christians including myself are guilty of having one.

My day at the clinic

It was most humiliating to be a child of God and walk into an abortion clinic.

Outside the facility were Christians with signs protesting against abortions. A woman pleaded with me saying "don't kill your baby." At that present time I was more afraid of the church folks killing me. You know, never hearing the end of it. I'd be (picked out to be the sermon of the month for the next nine months). In addition to that I was fearful of remaining on welfare along with not being able to go to college to better my life.

Not knowing whether I would live or die there was the concern of going to hell. {Sisters, Abortions are risky}! Because of this I prayed and asked God to have mercy on me. *Yes, I did!* To go on while waiting for my name to be called in the clinic, I noticed a Christian woman sitting next to me terrified, quietly praying (sounded like in tongues). I felt ashamed and helpless because I couldn't help her because we were both in the same *sin-ship!*

I began to pray again and vow to the Lord that if He delivered me I would serve him and never go back to that life again.

After the abortion was over I was so thankful to be alive and not in hell. To my surprise a young sister I knew was laying in another bed across from me in the recovery room. She was one of the praise dancers from a former church. Neither one of us said, "Praise the Lord" under those circumstances. Starring at each other in shock, *we definitely didn't have to worry about discrediting one another!*

Being revealed to me years later: every time a woman has an abortion she's offering her seed (issue) as a blood sacrifice unto Molech (the fire God) worshiped with humans preferably a child, or baby born, or aborted. It really doesn't matter murder is murder. A life is a life and it begins at conception.

Leviticus 20:1-5 KJV
1 And the Lord spoke unto Moses, saying,
2 Again, thou shalt say to the children of Israel, or the strangers that sojourn in Israel, that giveth any of his <u>seed</u> unto Molech; he shall surely be put to death: the people of the land shall stone him with stones, 3 And I will set my face against that man, and will cut him off from among his people because he hath given of his seed unto Molech, to defile my sanctuary, and to profane my holy name. 4 And if the people of the land do any ways hide their eyes from the man, when he giveth of his seed unto Molech, and kill him not: 5 Then I will set my face against that man, and against his family and will cut him off, and all that go a whoring after him, to commit whoredom with Molech, from among their people.

As demonstrated in this scripture God did not take murdering babies or children lightly. The ones responsible were punishable by the death sentence. In addition to that, abortion releases murder. *It could just be murdering with the tongue!*

If we confess our sins He is faithful and just to forgive us our sins and to cleanse us from all unrighteousness. 1John 1:9 KJV

To God be the Glory! Repenting is not a bad thing either, Amen!

Masturbation

Many men and women use God as a crutch or an excuse to sin. Becoming defensive they often argue that God understands my weaknesses. He knows that I have needs; remember Jesus was a human also.

Sooo……, instead of fornicating they masturbate. Uh Oh! (Oh yes I'm going there). Countless single men and women are truly convinced that they are not troubling anyone by doing this activity. They assume they could be doing worse things such as fornicating.

Yes, it may bring temporary relief and gratification but masturbating is a sin issue. Furthermore every time an individual indulges in this act they are releasing spirits, including rape spirits on another person. The one doing it I can guarantee that they are 95% of the time meditating on someone else while performing the sexual act. *Masturbation is hypnotic!*

Many fellow Christians have confessed to me about their torments. They expressed that: they felt helpless at night or even during the day. It felt as if the person was right there violating them.

Yes, there are sex demons that do attack at night. But here I am not referring to them but to those individuals deliberately masturbating and astro projecting him/or herself on another individual. This will cause ones life to be a living nightmare.

Let's use Jalisa, (All the names have been changed to protect their privacy).

Jalisa is a 37 year old woman. She's been dating a Born again Christian man named Joe for about 5 years. Joe for some reason or another just would not commit to Jaliasa. (Christian men play games and so do some women). Jaliasa was heart broken over and over again. You think it would be enough to walk away, no! There were soul ties and Joe had a secret, a masturbating problem. Oh yes, **good people, anointed nice people struggle with masturbation!**

At three or four in the morning, Jaliasa could feel Joe thinking about her while he masturbated. She felt the actual sensation of intercourse. Jaliasa tried to confront Joe but Joe maintained that he was doing nothing wrong. Her response was I could feel what you're doing and it's very disturbing. The only release from this was asking God to convict him to make them stop. This went on for years and one day ceased. Joe was delivered.

Masturbation is abuse in the spirit against another individual's will. *Repeating again, it is spiritual rape.*

God's Word says in Matt. 5:28 if a man looks at a woman to lust after her, he commits adultery in his heart.

Masturbation is sin period! *So stop it if that's you!* It is better to marry than to burn (with lust or in *hell*).

Saints that have fallen into traps of fornication are encouraged to just walk away from it; easy "yeah right". From experience, we know that it is not that simple. First, you have ties in the physical, emotional, mental (soul ties). Desiring to Get out of ungodly relationships may mean bondage until every tie is cut and severed. Sex including masturbation is not only fleshly but very emotional, mental as well as spiritual.

Satan is able to keep many in bondage because he plays the same episodes over and over again in ones mind. He places strongholds of wickedness in ones mind and than matches the appropriate emotion to the flesh.

If an individual does not know any better they will entertain the thoughts and then perform the act. Being emotional and not led by the spirit can keep one from remaining free and out of the wilderness of sin.

2 Corinthians 10:4-5 KJV
4 For the weapons of our warfare are not carnal, but mighty through God to the pulling down of strongholds;
(words or images)
5 Casting down imaginations…
These are (images that Satan is recording and in the minds to persuade and convince many to disobey and fall. Through Gods power one is able to tear down Satan's Kingdom of thoughts, image words, and emotional impressions in ones soul and mind.

God's Word and Power will bring every disobedient thought into captivity and place it under arrest through the believer.

Pray this prayer
Lord forgive me for sinning against you and against my body. I repent of all lust, adultery and fornication. Help me to forgive myself. Lord I let this mind be in me that was also In Christ Jesus. Give me a mind to turn away from being perverse, a fornicator, masturbator, a reader, a viewer or participant of porn material. (Including phone sex)! Let my eye be single for you that my whole body will be full of light in Jesus name. Jesus I know the truth and I am being set free right now. Help me to come out of every Ungodly relationship help me to live holy. Lord, thoroughly cleanse me and keep me.

Celibacy   (A gift or a curse)
Oftentimes when individuals mention the word celibacy or eunuch (Matthew 19:12) their general response is "God did not give me that gift". "I'm a real man or/I'm a real woman"! Well the thing about it is no one was born married. Marriage and its benefits is a desire and a gift. For we need for the natural body food, clothing and shelter.
On the other hand Lust is a deadly craving not a need! You won't physically die if you abstain from sex, but in some cases you can die from having sex with disease

infected partners!

All believers (single or married) have the gift of (celibacy). That is the ability to with stain from sex, but every believer is not a (eunuch) an individual that chooses not to have sex for life for various reasons.

The adversary tries hard to give mankind his curses of promiscuity. His goal is to contaminate the gift. Much of the time it is allowed to happen because one doesn't know how to use and release their gift. Going through in the flesh is not the excuse or reason to fornicate or commit adultery. It is a reason to learn how to draw from the gift of celibacy and self control (temperance). It is the time of living and waiting in *victory!*

Many go through in their flesh because the adversary moves in their dreams, emotions, mind, and addition to using others peoples projected lusts and issues.

James 1:14-15 KJV
14 But every man is tempted, when he is drawn away of his own lust, and enticed. 15 Then when lust has conceived, it bringeth forth sin, when it is finished it bringeth forth death.

Satan desires for believers to get involved in ungodly relationships to spiritually impregnate them with lustful seeds. This is in order that they will crave other lustful experiences. These demon seeds hide in sexual organs waiting for opportunities to manifest.

Many in bondages are bound due to previous relationship soul ties that have not been properly severed. To go on if those spirits that were transferred are not completely cast out, the individual will continue to crave and lust.

Furthermore the individual needs to arrest the spirits and forbid their operations. (To be discussed further in a later chapter).

A Prayer for deliverance

Father in the name of Jesus I cast out my temple every demon issue that was deposited in me during every ungodly sexual relationship. I burn every ungodly soul tie. We also burn and sever physical, mental, sexual, emotional ties, from every ungodly past relationship in the name of Jesus. Lord you said that whatever I bind and declare unlawful or improper on earth it is what you already bound in heaven.

The seal of the Holy Ghost and the blood of Jesus gives me this power and authority. I now take authority today over every masturbating, fornicating, lustful spirit, as well as perverse spirit (human or demon spirit). From this day on you are under Holy Ghost arrest. You will never ever attack or torment me again in the name of Jesus. The struggle is over forever!

"Tell fornication, and lust to rest in peace forever! (AMEN)"

Chapter 11

Airway And Territorial Spirits

S atan is the master concerning the airway. The scripture says that he is the prince and power of the air. He regulates and rules the airway like the government rules the natural airway for airplanes, and jets etc. In addition to setting up demon stations to make mans life a living nightmare. To go on he uses principalities, powers as well as spiritual wickedness to hinder man.

Daniel 10:12-13 KJV

12 Then said he unto me, Fear not, Daniel: for from the first day that thou didst set thine heart to understand, and to chasten thyself before thy God, thy words were heard, and I am come for thy words. 13 But the *prince* of the Kingdom of Persia withstood me one and twenty days: but, lo Michael one of the chief princes, came to help me; and I remained there with the kings of Persia.

**Prince is referring to a spiritual principality.

One thing I learned about territorial spirits is that when they position themselves in a specific location they are guaranteed a body.

These spirits claim cities, impoverished neighborhoods, wealthy neighborhoods, bars, schools, malls. To go on, movie theaters, night clubs, apartment complexes, communities and churches. They love crowds because they are guaranteed a body.

I oftentimes ride on the trains in NYC many times feeling great. Later during the ride if there was demonic activity on the train I would began to feel weak, heavy, drained, or even sleepy for no reason. After leaving the train an hour or so I later began to feel better.

Ladies have you ever went shopping and felt an excitement about it. The moment you entered a particular department store your head started pounding. You remembered the migraine you had the last three times you went into that same store. Deciding to end your shopping experience and go home. Upon going home you felt fine. For years this would happen to me when I went into certain supermarkets. I thought it was just me or the light or just something in the air. I began to pay attention realizing that these were territorial spirits releasing the spirit of infirmity.

Territorial spirits generally do not leave with the person it attacks (but sometimes they do). These temporary vessels are used while in the territorial boundary. When that body leaves, they hop on the next victim.

Many cities are metropolis for territorial demons. Infestations of drugs, alcohol, habits, poverty, welfare is prevalent. To go on crimes, depression, high school dropouts low achievers as well as no achievers.

Children in the inner city really suffer because of lack of prayer in the school. This an open door for spiritual strongholds. Having school age children we can identify with the negative results of no prayer in school. Sam the youngest of my three children often shared with me her experiences. Often she complained of headaches, lack of focus, and concentration in certain classrooms as well as hallways. Being curious if it was just something she was imagining. She began questioning other children to see if they suffered from headaches also while in school. Almost every child she interviewed responded with, *"yes, they have"!* When Sam attended elementary school in Brooklyn there were fights everyday on the same corner with different children.

Some neighborhoods you hear in the news relentlessly always the same crimes, of shootings, murders, rape, drugs etc.

We will not exempt Houses of God from territorial demons. They station in churches because they are guaranteed a body. They influence and cause confusion, gossip, debate to shoot down the pastor, saints, and ministry. Their ultimate plan is to hinder and distract the anointing from flowing. These spirits love to sit in specific seat areas. When the individual sits there they often take on the characteristic of that demon. This really destroys ministries.

Prayer, praise, fasting, repenting addition to casting them out is essential to break the power over every territorial spiritual stronghold in the church.

Deliverance And Purging!

16 John answered, saying unto them all, I indeed baptize you with water; but one mightier that I cometh, the latchet of whose shoes I am not worthy to unloose: he shall baptize you with the Holy Ghost and with fire; 17 Whose fan is in his hand, and he will thoroughly purge his floor, and will gather the wheat into his garner: but the chaff he will burn with fire unquenchable.

Luke 3:16-17 KJV

Chapter 12

Somebody Lied To You!

St. John 5:2-9 KJV
2 Now there is at Jerusalem by the sheep market a pool, which is called in the Hebrew tongue Bethesda, having five porches. 3 In these lay a great multitude of impotent folk, of blind, halt, withered, waiting for the moving of the water, For an angel went down at a certain season into the pool, and troubled the water: whosoever then first after the troubling of the water stepped in was made whole of whatsoever disease he had. 5 And a certain man was there,

which had an infirmity thirty and eight years. 6 When Jesus saw him lie, and knew that he had been now a long time in that case, he saith unto him, Wilt thou be made whole? 7 The impotent man answered him, Sir, I have no man, when the water is troubled, to put me into the pool: but while I am coming another stepped down before me.

The No Man Syndrome

I have no man to lay hands on me! I have no man to encourage me! I have no man to help me because I'm sick! I'm poor! I don't have a husband! Blah! Blah! Blah!

These are some of the biggest lies and excuses that Satan has used on Gods people including myself. Lying, dependent spirits need to be confronted in every believer's life.

It took at least 10 or more years to get my healings as well as deliverances. The reason; I was waiting for the right man to lay hands on me.

Coming from a Pentecostal background I observed that the majority of the ministries attended then believed in laying on of hands. Many treated the gift as if it were a magic wand or something.

Mark 16:17 KJV says:

And these signs shall follow them that believe; In my name shall they cast out devils; they shall speak with new tongues;

Often this verse is interpreted incorrectly. It did not say these signs shall follow the *preacher* the *pastor* or *the mother of the church*. It did not say these signs shall follow them that are delivered and have it all together and that are trying. It says these signs shall follow them that <u>believe.</u> I was a believer, a believer with issues but a believer.

Mark 10:50-52 KJV:

50 And he, casting away his garment, rose, and came to Jesus. 51 And Jesus answered and said unto him, <u>What wilt thou that I should do unto thee?</u> The blind man said unto

him, Lord, that I might receive my sight. 52 And Jesus said unto him, Go thy way; thy faith hath made thee whole. And immediately he received his sight, and followed Jesus in the way.

This man was blind, Jesus knew he was blind. He didn't ask for his resume' or cover letter. He did not harass him about his doctrine or church membership; He wasn't interrogated on how many years he was saved or how he or his momma must have messed up. No! Jesus asked him a simple question what can I do for you. "Lord I want to see." Immediately he received his sight because of his *faith.*

The scripture cannot be broken. In other words it has the same meaning and it will work the same even for demons that need to be kicked out or cast out of a believer's life. For with man it is impossible but with God all things are possible.

Jesus is asking the same questions *"What can I do for you? Will you be made whole? Will you be delivered?"* You can lay hands on that condition yourself and command those demons that are tormenting you to come out of you. Stop waiting on a man. Know you not that you are the temple of the Holy Ghost. Satan's demons have no right to be in your temple. ***Kick them out yourself In The Name Of Jesus!***

Chapter 13

Signs To Look
For Prior To Deliverance!

There are many expressed outward and inward signs to show that a person is being contaminated by demon(s):

1 In the eyes

Involuntary movements, blinking, squinting, or poor focal concentration is common. To continue, a sensation of ones eyes bulging out, dizziness or blurriness. Some of this one might experience upon entrance of a contaminated room or viewing contaminated TV shows, movies, as well as videos. But God is a deliverer!

2 In the nose
Feeling congested continuously, a sniffing sensation, quizzing, sneezing and funny movement with nose while the anointing is going forth during service. But God is a deliverer

3 In the throat
An inability to clear throat a blockage of mucus plugs, or gravel in throat, a interference in speaking and singing certain notes, coughing, choking.

4 In the mouth
Involuntarily talking, gnashing of teeth, screaming, cursing or talking jittery. Talking about killing or hurting oneself or some one else. God is a deliverer

5 In the muscles and joints
A weight or heaviness on shoulders and neck extending from head. A Tightness, stiffness, inflicting pain in joints in the legs or arms. God is a deliverer

6 In the bones
Involuntary movements or shaking. This often happens during deliverance services. A person may fall out and start shaking profusely. The unclean spirit is fighting to come out and they are being removed from the bone marrow through the anointed Word of God. See Hebrews 4:12.

7 In the legs and arms
Involuntary movements, painful cramping in legs, arms, ankles, and sexual organs are often common.

8 In the stomach
A person may feel as if a ball or something is moving around

or jerking around in their belly. Feeling bloated, or full without eating. This may interfere with eating, retaining food, and gaining weight, causing nausea.
But God is a deliverer!

9 In the chest area
Sometimes spirits will manifest by causing It may be very disturbing when wearing something tight!
But God is a deliverer!

10 In the head
A Sensation of strange movements, pressure, tightness, stiffness or a discomfort in head area, But God is a deliverer!

11 In the mind
Feeling tormented, inability to focus, concentrate, unsoundness, confusion, mental monstrous, demonic, animal images, and disturbing voices. But God is a deliverer!

12 In the nerves
Restless, cannot sleep, experiencing shakes, cannot relax or sit still for prolonged periods of time, nightmares.

I suffered from nightmares for years. At one time I thought they would never end. The devil is a liar. One day I made a choice that I would never again have nightmares, because God's Word declares I can have what I say.
But God is a deliverer!

Psalm 3:8 KJV
8 I will both lay me down in *peace*, and *sleep*: for thou, Lord, only makest me dwell in safety.

Chapter 14

The Urgency Of Deliverance.
{Be Careful!}

1 Thessalonians 5:23 KJV
And the very God of peace sanctify you wholly; and I pray God your whole spirit and soul and body be preserved blameless unto the coming of our Lord Jesus Christ.

Be careful that you aren't caught up in getting delivered that you try to do it yourself. God will sanctify you or purge you if you let him. He will step back if you try to do it yourself.

Suggestions for receiving a rapid deliverance!

- *Accepting Jesus as your Lord and Savior!*

- *Be willing to be teachable and willing to surrender. (Being teachable will make you reachable)*

- *Fast, and pray.*

- *Knowledge of the Word.*

- *Faith to believe!*

- *Repenting- demons will leave more rapidly when you are completely submitted to God.*

- *Resistance against the enemy (Fight do not accept anything the Devil says).*

- *Knowledge of deliverance.*

- *Obedience.*

- *Attend an anointed Bible teaching, preaching, deliverance ministry regularly!*

Chapter 15

Purging! (The Purification Process)

Purging is one the most important parts of a deliverance. Understand this, the Lord wants his people completely whole and it is nothing to be ashamed of! God does not give out band-aids neither is he a fixer upper; he makes individuals completely whole and clean.

*1 **Preachers, pastors, ministers,** and **praise singers** purge whenever they minister under the fire of the Holy Ghost. Many are ashamed and embarrassed to do it. Yet I have seen many use their hanky's for their issues. Purging releases the flow of the anointing. It removes blockages, and dams while enabling the anointing to flow from their bellies. (It's a good thing).*

*2 **Casting demons out by the anointing and spoken Word,** Matthew 15:22-28 or laying on of the hands will cause purging and foaming of the mouth in the individual, Luke 9:39, Mark 16:17*

*3 **Layman saints** purge when they receive the anointed Word. Whenever revival is taking place in you, bring your tissues for your issues.*

*4 **When a person tarries** to receive the infilling of the Holy Ghost he/or she might purge during, before or after the filling.*

~Water in the Bible~

Luke 3:16-17 KJV:

16 John answered, saying unto them all, *I indeed baptize you with water;* but one mightier than I cometh, the latchet of whose shoes I am not worthy to unloose: he shall baptize you with the Holy Ghost and fire: 17 Whose fan is in his hand, and he will thoroughly *purge* his floor, and will gather the wheat into his garner; but the chaff he will burn with fire unquenchable.

I am going to focus verse on 16. John in the 16th verse baptized his disciples with water to prepare for the in filling of the Holy Ghost. Water is also used for preparation of deliverance and purging. It gives God something to work with other than faith and repentance.

Fire

He shall baptize you with the Holy Ghost and Fire!

Fire is used for many things such as cooking, heating, burning, refining metal and gold to make it pure and more valuable. The Fire of the Holy Ghost was not only given to make us shout, speak in tongues, preach, teach, or comfort us. There is a part of the Holy Spirit that was given to us to refine us to purify us to make us more valuable for his service. This is done by removing spiritual chaff imparted by demonic impartation.

Fiery Tongues

Are also for purging,
Let me show you what happened on the day of Pentecost.

Acts 2:1-4 KJV
1 And when the day of Pentecost was
fully come, they were all with one accord in one place. 2 And suddenly there came a sound from Heaven as of a rushing mighty wind, and it filled all the house where they were sitting.3 And there appeared unto them cloven tongues like as of fire, and it sat upon each of them. 4 And they were all filled with the Holy Ghost. And began to speak with other tongues as the spirit gave them utterance.
This was the beginning of the purifying process!

Holy Ghost fiery tongues will thoroughly purge His floor. Well our body is the temple of His floor. Purging and rebuking spirits can be also be accomplished when one sings and prays in tongues.

Because tongues are a gift from God it is freely given. Some of the purposes it was given is to help us to fight, edify, or build us up, in addition to cleanse. He gives us power to be more like Himself holy, blameless, and without demon issues.

Cleaning

An example of cleaning or purging:
I was in a service one day and I began to speak in anointed tongues and give a word under the unction of the Holy Ghost that God was cleaning his people. While this was taking place a woman fell out under the power of God and began to throw up white foam.

The people did not understand that deliverance was taking place. They thought that a spirit had jumped on her. No it was just the opposite demons were coming out of the woman.

There are different tongues:

Tongues of men
(languages) examples: Spanish, French, and Latin etc. Genesis 11:1 Acts 2:3-6, 1 Corinthians 13:1

New tongues or unknown tongues
Heavenly tongues, (for the believers only but after Pentecost). For prayer building, anointing building, (see Jude 20) also to receive and speak mysteries and revelation. 1 Cor. 14:2 (they are non earthly tongues, non angelic tongues) Isaiah 50:4 Mark 16:17,

Divers tongues
The supernatural empowerment to speak in other unlearned languages including, earthly, angelic or new tongues. This is called the special gifts of tongues. 1 Cor. 12:10

Tongues of Angels
1 Corinthians 13:1 KJV
Though I speak with the tongues of men and of angels, and have not charity, I am become as a sounding brass, or a tinkling cymbal.

The writer Paul of Corinthians made a statement about his ability to speak in angelic tongues. Angelic language is also a heavenly language (but before Pentecost).

Well Satan and his imps are fallen angels; do you think he forgot the angelic language? I don't think so. The gift of speaking in angelic languages can give individuals ability to communicate with their own angels. This would prove to be helpful. At the same time rebuke evil angels that are unseen in which are attacking them!

Praise
And Deliverance

Praise The Lord !

"Enter his gates with thanksgiving, and into his courts with praise: be thankful unto him and bless his name."

Psalm 100:4 KJV

Chapter 16

Using Praise To Receive Deliverance!

Praise can also be used for deliverance purposes. Merriam Webster's Collegiate Thesaurus gives these definitions for **Praise:** To bless, celebrate, cry up, eulogize, extol, glorify, hymn. Laud, magnify, and panegyrize, psalm, psalmody, resound.

When you praise God, you are blessing him, by way of having a celebration of his goodness in your spirit, soul and body. When you celebrate you might dance, jump, kick, sing, run, laugh, or shout!

{You can direct your praise to receive what you need from God}

Here are a few benefits in praising God,

Praise empowers:
Anointed Worship leaders empower the saints to praise and do service by stirring up the gifts in the congregation.

Healing:
There was a crippled beggar at the gate called beautiful that was healed by the power of God when Peter ministered a word of healing to him.

Acts 3:6-8 (KJV)
Then Peter said, Silver and gold have I none; but such as I have give I thee: In the name of Jesus Christ of Nazareth rise up and walk 7 And he took him by the right hand, and lifted him up and immediately his feet and ankle bones received strength. 8 And he leaping up stood, and walked, and entered with them into the temple, walking, an leaping and praising God.

Deliverance cleansing:
I have been to many anointed services and I have seen multitudes of people celebrate God in a dance, to jump, and shout to praise God. After which they would spit up issues during these yoke breaking services. Some people get so deep in God that their sophistication hinders them from getting free from issues. They feel that this is unnecessary. They do not understand that praising God is not just about making noise but making free.

Psalm 100:4 KJV
Enter into his gates with thanksgiving, and into his courts with praise: be thankful unto him and bless his name.
Praise is a garment a prerequisite to worship it is what we do

before worship (spiritual foreplay).

Praise will free one from the spirits of oppression, and heaviness:
Isaiah 61: 3 KJV
To appoint unto them that mourn in Zion, to give unto them beauty for ashes, the oil of joy for mourning, the garment of praise for the spirit of heaviness; they might be called trees of righteousness, the planting of the Lord, that he might be glorified.

Psalm 103:1 NIV
1 Praise the Lord, O my soul all my inmost being, praise his holy name.

When you praise God, you may cry up some things in the form of tears. Crying is a form of purging and it brings release in your innermost being.

Breakthrough and elevation:
Psalm 149:6-7 amp
6 Let the high praises of God be in their throats and a two edge sword in their hands. 7 To wreak vengeance upon the nations and chastisement upon the peoples, fetters of iron.

Because praise is a form of spiritual warfare, you can actually shout demons out.

Shabach: a loud sustaining noise, shout or praise. It will push ones praise and worship from the head, nasal, through the throat through the chest down to the river of ones belly. This force will fill ones belly with fire in which pushes out all demonic deposits. Furthermore praise releases the river of life that wants to flow in you and out of you. Hallelujah, Glory!

God is calling forth *balance* into his body. The church can not dispose of praise and replace it with worship. *Both* are needed and important or else He would not have put it in his Word. Praise is a commandment as well as requirement for worship. Psalm 150:6.

Praise can not be replaced with the word: for all things work together for good. God does not care about your position in the church or in life. It doesn't matter whether you're a doctor, lawyer, teacher, preacher, married rich or on welfare. Praise is vital. It is a weapon that cuts off the enemies air supply and sets one free!

(Judah means praise) Genesis 49:8 is a prophetic word to the sons of Israel (we are spiritual Israel)

Genesis 49:8 KJV
Judah, thou art he whom thy brethren shall praise; Thy hand shall be in the neck of thy enemies;...

Praise immobilizes, stills, silences, Satan and his imps:
Just think if he can be stilled and silenced in your circumstances than you will *be free. Your praise will do that for you.*

Warfare:
Psalm 8:2 KJV
Out of the mouth of babes and sucklings has thou ordained strength because of thine enemies, that thou mightest still the enemy and the avenger.

Psalm 8:2 NIV
2 From the lips of children and infants you have ordained praise, because of your enemies to silence the foe and the avenger.

Psalm 149:6-8 NIV
May the praise of God be in their mouths and a double edged sword in their hands, To inflict vengeance on the nations and punishment on the peoples. To bind their kings with fetters and nobles with shackles of iron,

Matthew 21:16 KJV

16. And said unto him, Hearest thou what these say? And Jesus saith unto them, Yea; have ye never read, Out of the mouth of babes and sucklings thou has ordained perfect praise.

Psalm 103:2 NIV

2 Praise the lord, O my soul forget not all his benefits.

Praising God will bring benefits in addition to purging your body and soul. The results will be more clarity to hear God. It gets the junk out of the trunk.

During the purging process, be patient; the more you learn about securing your deliverance the less often you will purge!

Praise
And
Deliverance!

continued.....

A Praise Exercise

Chapter 17

Praise and Deliverance!
(A Praise Exercise)

Praising is self-help for the believer to obtain their deliverance.

By directing ones praise deep down to the belly; it will push out anything blocking the flow of the anointing. Before you even began a prayer is needed to ask assistance from the Holy Spirit. This will release His anointing with fire to purge.

A prayer for deliverance

Father in the name of Jesus; Lord I need you to deliver me today because I can't do it alone. Lord I thank you for delivering me now, because I have a blood brought right to be free.

Lord let your Holy Ghost fire thoroughly purge me from the spiritual chaff (the demons issues) from the crown of my head to the soles of my feet.

Let your anointing for my deliverance cover every area including: My head, my eyes, my mind, my nose, my ears, neck, shoulders, arms, wrists fingers, toes and all my upper extremities as well as lower extremities.

Lord let the fire of God thoroughly purge my blood, bone marrow, bones, joints, muscles, heart, lungs, liver, and sexual organs. Every tissue and cell in my body I command right now to be free now in Jesus name!

I thank you lord for being my helper as well as deliverer. Amen!

~Preparation~

Before you praise

1. Dedicate at least 1/2-2 hours daily to praise and worship in order to obtain your deliverance. You may need more than one session to build up strength especially it you are not used to praise and worship in this kind of way. Please continue to do this until you are free.

2. Invest in anointed fiery praise CD's or DVD's. Play them while you are doing the exercise to (create the atmosphere for deliverance).

3. Fast for this day, Isaiah 58:3-6

4 Water will aid you during your deliverance. It's easier to have a wet deliverance rather than dry.

5. If possible, have another anointed Christian assist you.

~A Praise~
~Session~

Begin to call on Jesus, the blood of Jesus, or hallelujah etc. Place your hand on your belly while calling on Jesus with a deep praise until you can feel some thing happening in the pit of your belly. Do it several times. One Important thing be persistent. ***Don't listen to the enemy!*** He will tell you that it is not going to work or you're not anointed enough or I'm not leaving. Some days you can just sing a song. I love you lord or any praise song will do. Hold the note until you feel pressure in your belly area. For example: J--e--s--u--s. In the beginning it may seem annoying and tiresome. It may even hurt while pushing the praise down to your belly.

Often times if there are intruders in your belly or (body) they may ball up in the corner and you may even gag a little.

Do not get discouraged; continue on for the ½ hour escalating eventually to an hour or two.

The more sessions you do the clearer your head, throat, chest and belly area will become. This will result in your deliverance. Finally, put the issues in the paper tissues, Finally, maintain a life style of worship and praise.

Chapter 18

After You Have Praised And Purged!

A fter you have purged you may see in the tissue, stool or bucket, different things. It might appear like mucus, jelly or a white foamy substance. God spoke to me about what this was, revealing that these are the unclean spirits that have mixed with the chemicals in your body producing this substance.

Furthermore when a person is being filled with the Anointed Word of He explained to me that the fire of the Holy Ghost removes spirits manifesting in white foam, mucus or jelly out of the blood, bone marrow, etc. Never force it. Wait on his anointing and let God do it!

Hebrew 4:12 KJV
For the word of God is quick and powerful and sharper than any two edge sword, piercing even to the dividing asunder of soul and spirit, and of the joints and marrow, and is a discerner of the thoughts and intents of the heart.

When the anointed word goes forth it will bring forth deliverance and freedom. I believe this is what the old mothers meant when they said loose here Satan. Demon Issues are being loosed from the bone marrow, blood, joints and, tissues.

Deliverance can be very uncomfortable especially if demons have been there a very long time. They might even try to fight to hold on. They do not have a choice but to come out at the commandment of an anointed believer in the name of Jesus.

This is my experience during the years as well observation viewing others going through the purification process.

1. After purging the mucus, jelly or white foam, the individual may feel sore and weak all over (as if someone has beaten them up on the inside). This feeling may come especially from the bones, muscle, and joints. Well you just came out of battle and guess what you're winning the war.
2. Some times the person will shake as if they were going into a convolution. The revelation the Lord gave me is that these spirits were in the body so long that the body went into shock. The spirits that were attached are finally being removed.

Mark 9:17-20 KJV
17 And one of the multitude answered and said, Master I have brought unto thee my son, which have a dumb spirit; 18

And whosesoever he taketh him, **he teareth him**: **and he foamed,** and gnashed with his teeth, and pineth away: and I spake to thy disciples that they should cast him out; but they could not. 19 He answered him, and saith O faithless generation, how long shall I be with you? How long shall I suffer you? Bring him unto me. 20 And they brought him unto him: and when he saw him, straightway the spirit tare him and he fell on the ground, and wallowed foaming. 21 And he asked his father, How long is it ago since this came unto him. <u>And he said since of a child.</u>

Mark 9:25-26 KJV

25 When Jesus saw that the people came running together he rebuked the foul spirit, saying, Thou dumb and deaf spirit I charge thee, Come out of him and enter into him no more. 26 The spirit cried and rent him sore, and came out of him: and he was as one dead: in so much that many said, He is dead, But Jesus took him by the hand and, lifted him up: and he arose.

Verse 25 Says that Jesus rebuked the spirit as soon as he saw the crowd coming. (I believe it was because demons love crowds and entertainment).

Verse 26 speaks about restoration the man appeared to be dead but Jesus took him by the hand and lifted him up; and he arose.

Individuals after massive deliverances need prayer to be restored, built up, including trust, dreams, the will to fight and live. Jesus lifted him, and the man arose. We also need to lift one another up in love.

Final thought about purging; do not believe the lie that the devil has told the body of Christ that we don't need to purge. That's was for grandma's time. After all, we are too sophisticated and educated to go through the motions of deliverance.

Darling, Sweet heart you are a target for issues if you live in crowded cities like New York, Chicago, Philadelphia, LA etc. You can pick up other peoples issue spirits by just being in the shopping malls, grocery stores, restaurants or workplaces. Not forgetting about you'll country folks you have easy access just by picking up the telephone or turning on the TV.

Maintaining Your Deliverance from.... Issues!

"Yet the Lord is faithful, and He will strengthen [you] and set you on a firm foundation and guard you from the evil [one]."

2 Thessalonians 3:3 amp.

Chapter 19

Obedience!

Ones blessings, deliverances, as well as victories are locked into obedience to the will of God. Obeying and submitting to God may not always suggest witnessing or preaching on the corner. It's the simple things such as obedience and submission to leadership. This will cover you as well as protect you.

He may also tell you to stop watching a TV program or don't pick up the telephone today or only talk on it for only 15 minutes. Or just simply apologize to someone that you've offended. Staying free from issues may mean making better choices and decisions by consulting God in every thing.

Proverbs 3:6-8 KJV
In all thy ways acknowledge him, and he shall direct thy paths. 7 Be not wise in thine own eyes but fear the lord and depart from evil. 8 It shall be health to thy navel and marrow to thy bones.

When a person learns who they are in Christ and understands the truth about issues in their tissues. Spirits will fall off of them without even trying too hard.

2 Corinthians 10:3-6 KJV
3 For though we walk in the flesh, we do not war after the flesh: 4 For the weapons of our warfare are not carnal, but mighty through God to the pulling down of strong holds; 5 Casting down imaginations and every high thing that exalts itself against the knowledge of God, and bringing into captivity every thought to the obedience of Christ; 6 _And having in a readiness to revenge all disobedience, when your obedience is fulfilled._

In other words insubordinate demons will become more subject to you because of your obedience to Christ. Jesus was not just glorified merely because he was Jesus, but because he was obedient to the cross and death assignments. Your personal submission will free you as well as release you from issues. And guess what it won't take that long.

Baggage Issues!

Here is a scenario:
Your assets are frozen and have now become your liability;
don't you think it's time for you to get rid of your issues?

Chapter 20

Baggage Issues!

S piritual baggage: can be trust issues, unforgiveness, yesterdays manna, old ways of doing things and *more!* God wants to do a new thing to give us new results that He may be glorified.

Release your Baggage!

Isaiah 43:18-19 KJV
Remember not the former things neither consider the things of old. 19 Behold I will do a new thing, now it shall spring

forth; shall ye not know it? I will even make a way in the wilderness, and rivers in the desert.

During the years I have received many Rhema Words that the Lord is going to bring restoration to my life.

Reflecting on the old manna, I would hold God as if he was my prisoner or hostage to my old way of doing things. I would not release God in my life because of my disappointments and hurts to do a new thing in the way of restoration. {I was real angry with God}

Now there are different meanings to restoration one is having something old and using modern technology to restore as close as possible to the original state. Examples might be: an old landmark building, antique jewelry, music from old 45 and 33 LPs.

Another meaning is to get back, or fill up like a store or stock room with new material that is marketable for today.

God wants to replenish, restore, restock, and refill our lives with new material. The reason is, what worked in the 70's, 80's, or 90's or even last year is not necessarily required for the present. Because God is an awesome God, he likes us to be in awe of Him bringing us out.

Trust Issues

Spiritual baggage can also be trust issues. Everyone you confided in has hurt you and now you're unable to trust anyone including God. You repel even the good away from you.

A person with trust issues is often paranoid, critical, fault finding, and judgmental. It is difficult for God to operate through them because faith, trust, as well as believing are closely correlated.

The more resentful, hateful and bitter they become the more they hinder their own faith from operating. The problem is not God but the individual with trust issues. They continue to encircle a wilderness of unforgiveness.

Un-forgiveness and your issues

Un-forgiveness can be one of the greatest obstacles in receiving and maintaining ones complete deliverance. This is a big door for the Devil to bring in depression, oppression, fear and other spirits. (They will leave and continue to come back if one doesn't release the baggage).

Individuals that view through the eyes of resentment are influenced by their un-forgiving heart. Their thoughts and choices are contaminated with negative venom. They often hold grudges and find it difficult to release the individuals that have wronged them. *Many just do not know how.* Now added to their un-forgiveness issues is judgment and retribution issues.

Math 7:1 amp
Do Not Judge and criticize and condemn others, so that you may not be judged and criticized and condemned yourselves.

Romans 12:19 amp
Beloved, never avenge yourself, but leave the way open for [Gods] wrath; for it is written, Vengeance is Mine, I will repay (requite) says the lord.

Romans 12:21 amp
Do no not let yourselves be overcome by
evil, but overcome (master) evil with good.

➤ How do we release un-forgiveness from out of our lives?

Luke 6:37-38 amp
37 Judge not [neither pronouncing judgment nor subjecting to censure]. And you will not be judged, do not condemn and pronounce guilty; and you will not be condemned and pronounced guilty; acquit and forgive and release (give up resentment, let it drop), and you will be acquitted forgiven and released.

➢ Get out of the judgment chambers!

Stop waiting for a judgment or revenge for your losses or hurts. Get off the judgment seat let God be God!

➢ Drop it, give up resentment and acquit the one offending you!

One Friday evening during a prayer meeting in my home a question came up. When you forgive a person do you have to forget? I don't believe that you can ever forget the wrong that was done to you, but I do believe that you can change how you respond to the wrong. I searched in the thesaurus the meanings of resentment. Animosity and ill will were some of the words that I found.

Animosity: is someone holding a grudge.

Ill Will: is having a sick will towards the person that has offended you.

In other words you are wishing evil on the individual. Because an unforgiving heart is a heart that is sick he is unable to operate in perfect love. God wants us to walk in love and bless those who hurt us and wrongfully use us.

Ephesians 4:26 KJV
Be ye angry, and sin not let not the sun go down upon your wrath.

To keep from responding to your hurts the remedy is to submit your thoughts, emotions and will to God. Ask him to cleanse you from all unrighteous.

➢ Now let it go!

Ask God to forgive you for holding on to it.

Confess that you forgive them, {even if you have to do it more than one hundred times a day.} Romans 10:9.

If we confess our sins, he is faithful and just to forgive us of our sins and cleanse us from all unrighteousness. I John 1:9 KJV

Matthew 18:21-22 KJV
21 Then came Peter to him, and said, Lord, how oft shall my brother sin against me, and I forgive him till seven times? 22 Jesus saith unto him, I say not unto thee, Until seventy times seven.

Even as confession is made unto salvation; confession is also made *rock solid* unto forgiveness.

➢ Release it to God and walk in love.

Walking in love does not necessarily mean that one is emotionally tied to or even likes the person.

Let me give you an example:
While we were in sin God did not like us but he yet loved us. He displayed this love by forgiving, and dying for us.

Romans 5:7-8 KJV
7 For scarcely for a righteous man will one die: yet peradventure for a good man some would even dare to die.
8 But God commendeth his love toward
us, in that, while we were yet sinners, Christ died for us.

Love is an action word, a giving word not always a huggy word. Being a Christian one is empowered by Christ to love everyone although one may not necessarily like them.
This love walk is a giving walk, faith walk, as well as choice walk. Because of this one is able to love unconditionally, forgive as well as be a blessing to their

enemies.

Romans 12:20-21 KJV
Therefore if thine enemy hunger, Feed him; if he thirst, give him drink for in so doing thou shall heap coals of fire on his head. 21 Be not overcome of evil, but overcome evil with good.

One way an individual will recognize if they are walking in forgiveness is when they no longer hear the persons that have wronged them constantly in their conversations. Healing will take time but God does not want individuals to hurt others with their tongue during the process. Unfreeze your assets by releasing your past issues!

A Prayer of forgiveness
First of all Lord, forgive me for being angry with you. Lord I forgive my friends, enemies, family as well as church members that have hurt and wronged me. Lord forgive me for holding resentment, grudges, ill will and, judgment, over them. Lord you said in your word in Matthew 6:12, 14 if I forgave my debtors of their trust passes you would forgive mine. Lord, forgive me. Release me from others that have grudges, resentment and that are pronouncing judgments against me. Undo and release me from their thoughts, soulish prayers and psychic powers to will to harm me and all that concerns me. Father I truly forgive them now and I will not harbor any animosity in my heart towards them.

Who the son has therefore made free is free indeed. Lord, cleanse my cloudy distorted thinking. Lord, have mercy on me and rebuild my trust and lead me to individuals whom I can trust. Let me just chalk all what I been through for joy and experience. Thank you, Lord for setting me free.

From this day on I will be an instrument of love and your glory Amen! *Move on, live and receive your deliverance!*

Now forgive your self and do not allow the devil to use your conscience to beat you up, because there is therefore <u>now</u> no condemnation to them that are in Christ Jesus.

Receiving a <u>*word*</u> of forgiveness will bring healing spiritually, emotionally, physically, mentally as well as financially. Be open and allow the lord to do a new thing in you; Let his <u>*Issues*</u> *and blessing* flow to and from your life.

❖ *Release your Baggage today!*

Chapter 21

Lock The Door, Cancel The Assignments!

MY mother was a single parent of three. Often still at work when my brothers and I came from school. Because of this we became latch key kids at an early age. The first thing she taught us was how to use our keys and *lock the door*. She also instructed us not to open the door to any strangers to guard us against thieves and molesters. Her Promise was that "she would be home later. Jesus has did not leave us without keys or instructions to use. Reminding us that, *"He will also return"*!

Matthew 16:19 amp

19 I will give you the keys of the kingdom of heaven; and whatever you bind (declare to be improper and unlawful) on earth must be what is already bound in heaven; and whatever you loose (declare lawful) on earth must be what is already loosed in heaven.

Demons are similar to the strangers and thieves that my mother warned me about.

The thief comes to steal, kill, and destroy. This is iniquity or lawlessness and it is ramped on the earth. Our keys are our power and authority to enforce the laws of the kingdom of God. All we need to do is to follow the instructions to see what Heaven says about demon intruders. Well if you are a believer than the kingdom of God is in you. Please use your keys!

Whenever demons are cast out the door has to be shut and locked.

Luke 11:24-26 amp

24 When the unclean spirit has gone out of a person it roams through waterless places in search [of a place] of rest release refreshment, ease); and finding none it says, I will go back to my house from which I came. 25 And when it arrives, it finds [the place swept and put in order and furnished and decorated. 26 And it goes and brings other spirits, seven [of them], more than itself, and they enter in, settle down and dwell there; and the last state of that person is worse than the first.

Verse's 24-26 describes the unclean spirits modes of operations. They wonder or roam through waterless, dry places. When they find no resting place they go check out the old body. They find it swept and put in order, furnished and decorated.

The question comes to mind, how in the world are they able to see in the house with such detail unless the door is open. If you leave your natural home open how much greater is your spiritual home. You can pray till you are blue in the face; if you don't invest in good locks and use them it is hopeless.

While Jesus was on the earth as the Son of man and Son of God he illustrated how to use the keys to lock doors against the enemy.

Mark 9:25 amp

25 But when Jesus noticed that a crowd [of people] running together, He rebuked the unclean spirit, saying to it, You dumb and deaf spirit, <u>I charge you to come out of him and never go into him again.</u>

The assignment was now canceled on that man. We have the same authority to cancel assignments, close, and lock the door by commanding the demons not to enter or return!

Jesus spoke with his mouth and charged or commanded that the dumb and deaf spirit to be band from that man. That was an example of using the keys to the kingdom and sealing the individual's deliverance.

John 14:12 KJV

14 Verily, verily, I say unto you, He that believeth on me, the works that I do shall he do also; and greater works than these shall he do; because I go unto my Father.

If Jesus was here he would do the works but because he left and went to the Father he told the believers to do the works. This is the believer's legal right and responsibility.

Just as my mother told me and I tell my child when they enter and leave; *Jesus is telling his children.*

Use Your Keys And Lock The Door!

The Conclusion!

Revelation 1:8 KJV
I am Alpha and Omega the beginning and the ending, saith the Lord.......

"Out of the mouths of babes and unweaned infants You have established strength because of Your foes, that You might silence the enemy and the avenger." **Psalm 8:2 amp**

Chapter 22

You Have A Right To Remain Silent!
(Arresting Demons)

T he days of hitting and missing are over! Being bound up in sin is frustrating enough. What's more challenging is endeavoring to come out and stay out. Preachers are easy to inform you that you need to be delivered. Guess what? You already knew that.

You follow all the steps of repentance, including walking away from all types of sin. You fast and pray, practically bring your bed to church because you want more of God.

Every time you step away from sin the lustful spirit attacks again. The temptation from your old habits is at the door overwhelming, overpowering your soul. The Lord continues to have mercy. *You're grown tired of your own self, because you don't know what to do keep this from happening again!*

This has been the same story for years. Your plea to God is ***"Help Lord I'm tired of struggling"!***

Temptation

Living holy would be a breeze if we lived in a holy, issue free, crimeless environment. *(Heaven)!*

Every time a believer decides to give up sin Satan's Kingdom is threatened. (It's not about you)! He assigns spirits of temptation to seduce you, to discourage, and hinder. He often will make many believers feel so frustrated to the point that very the thing that they hate they now crave.

"Help Lord I need victory to live holy"! How can one do this? The solution, learn your rights and place every foul lawless spirit under Holy Ghost Arrest.

This chapter will discuss your authority as a believer and spiritual police officer on this earth. Turn to:

Matthew 18:18 KJV

Verily I say unto you, Whatsoever ye shall bind on earth shall be bound in heaven: and whatsoever ye shall loose on earth shall be Loosed in Heaven.

The King James Version expresses the laws of binding and loosing. I always interpreted this scripture to mean to pin down to immobilize. Through research I found that it meant a little more than that.

Matthew 18:18 amp
Truly I tell you, whatever you forbid and declare to be improper and unlawful on earth must be what is already forbidden in heaven and whatever you permit and declare proper and lawful on earth must be what is already permitted in heaven.

This binding was more referring to a legal binding contract or legal consent, declaration or permission. In Matthew 16:19 Jesus gave keys the legal authority or delegated permission to the church.

We also have been given delegated permission to use our binding (legal ability) to make spiritual arrests. Just as natural police officers have been given permission by the governor or mayor so do we by God.

The word arrest means to put an end to, to stop. We have a right to stop the enemy!

The Holy Ghost Restraint
2 Thessalonians 2:3, 6-7 amp
3 Let no one deceive or beguile you in any way, for that day will not come except the apostasy comes first [unless the predicted great falling away of those who have professed to be Christians has come], and the man of lawlessness (sin) is revealed, who is the son of doom (of; perdition),

6 And now you know what is restraining him [from being revealed at this time]; it is so that he; may be manifested (revealed) in his own (Appointed) time. 7 For the mystery of lawlessness (that hidden principle of rebellion against constituted authority) is already at work in the world, [but it is] restrained only until he who restrains is taking out of the way.

The Holy Spirit in operation through the believer is the restraining, stopping power (and it's still here). Believers have the constituted authority, the God given right to stop, still, as well as silence the enemy according to Psalm 8:2.

Demons study believers to observe whether they will entertain them, or read them their rights. We are to arrest them and never entertain them. Even as Jesus came to destroy the works of the devil by using his presence and authority so are we in this earth. Just as criminals run when they see the police, when we walk confident in our authority the demons will flee from us. We have the Holy Ghost restraining power as well as the legal binding contract of God's Word.

All we need to do is learn what the heavenly contract says and use that on earth to set ourselves free and than release others in bondage. Do not only cast the demons out, arrest the demons restrain them by the power of the Holy Ghost. Forbid their operation on this earth.

Many are tormented by the same demons. They cast them out they just come right back although many are living holy, (recycled issues). Why is that? The reason is because the enemy goes about as a roaring lion seeking whom he may devour and he devours *ignorance*!

You can stop depression by arresting the spirit! You can stop torment of the mind by arresting the spirit! Tell the enemy you will not use my body to fornicate, lust, sin, gossip, commit adultery, or masturbate.

Verbally arrest the spirits, and as previously mentioned in the last chapter lock the door by refusing to entertain them. Renounce sin! Place every foul spirit under Holy Ghost Arrest. In order to keep your deliverance you have to close every *ignorant, willful, and sinful* door. To go on further every disobedient door!

Stop acting like you don't know what to do when temptations knocks. Open up your big mouth before it comes with the confession of your faith. Tell those demons tormenting you, frustrating you that I place you under arrest by the Power of the Holy Ghost. You will never ever use my body or do that to me again. Glory!

Prayer and Confession

<u>Taking authority over the atmosphere</u>

Father; in the name of Jesus I thank you for this day. I am blessed and highly favored. I thank you for your provision, and protection body, mind, soul and spirit. More than anything lord I thank you that you have delivered me from the powers of darkness!

Colossians 2:13-15 amp

13 And you who were dead in trespasses and in the uncircumcision of your flesh (your sensuality, your sinful carnal nature), [God] brought to life together with [Christ], having [freely] forgiven us all our transgressions, 14 Having cancelled and blotted out and wiped away the hand writing of the note (bond) with its legal decrees and demands which was in force and stood against us (hostile to us). This [note with its regulations, decrees, and demands [He set a side and cleared completely out of out way by nailing it to [His] cross. 15 [God] disarmed the principalities and powers that were ranged against us and made a bold display and public example of them, in triumphing over them in Him and in it [the cross].

Because of this Lord I am free and have victory every where I go and everywhere I place my feet. I use my authority to come against all lawlessness of the devil in my life, my home, and everywhere on this earth in Jesus name. I am an heir of God and joint heir with Christ Jesus. All that Jesus has I have a blood brought right I also have it. I speak I have deliverance today and everyday. I take authority over the atmosphere and airway today and every day. I speak to every demon and unclean spirit that is trying to find my body or the body of my family members. You are forbidding to do so. I send every foul spirit to the foot of the cross that is attacking me. Declaring you to be unlawful; you are now bound and placed under Holy Ghost Arrest in Jesus name!

Territorial spirits have boundaries but we have the right to take the boundaries and claim them as territories for Gods kingdom,

Joshua 1:2-3 KJV
2 Moses my son is dead now therefore arise, go over the Jordan, thou, and all this people, unto the land which I do give to them, even to the children of Israel. 3 Every place that the sole of your foot shall tread upon, that have I given unto you, as I said unto Moses.

Establish your boundaries

In the name of The Lord Jesus Christ of Nazareth who came in the flesh, Satan, I establish my boundaries and your boundaries concerning me and my family. I decree that you and your demons, and powers are unlawful to come near my home, my church, businesses, and family in the name of Jesus. I declare according to Matthew 18:18 it is unlawful, illegal, and improper for you Satan and your demons to transfer, or exchange your filthy demons in me or any one of my family members or possessions. In Jesus name, I receive deliverance now. I have the right of Calvary's cross to be free from depression, oppression, and possessions of any kind. I know the Word Satan and the Son of God has truly made me free. All violators are now placed under arrest in Jesus name. I cast every foul spirit out now in Jesus name! I choose to stay free from torment, transference or exchange of any kind. I seal my entire home with the blood of Jesus from ceiling to floor from door to wall as well as all of my furniture and possessions. I charge the immediate atmosphere or airspace where I live or wherever I go with the blood of Jesus Christ and his anointed power in Jesus name. I have this blood brought right! 20 thousand or more warrior angels of God are standing guard of my home and community or wherever I go everyday in the name of Jesus. Demons are subject to me because my name is written in The Lambs Book of Life. Every time I enter a room, a bus, train, car, church or walk down a street I take authority over that airspace and claim it back to God in Jesus name. I decree great Blessings and Abundant Favor with God and man wherever I rest my feet forever in Jesus name. Amen!

Believing that you have been blessed by the reading material, I am also available for speaking engagements, women's conferences and or/workshops. Please send all inquires and correspondence to my email address: www.Godsplan4uminis@aol.com or view my website at: Issuesandyourtissues.net

And remember God loves you and
He Has A Plan 4U!

Evangelist V. Miller

***If you need additional copies of this book, you can purchase them at: lulu.com or have your local book store order them today!*

Notes

Notes

Notes

Notes

Notes

www.ingramcontent.com/pod-product-compliance
Lightning Source LLC
Chambersburg PA
CBHW021110090426
42738CB00006B/576